Past Masters
General Editor Keith Thomas

Petrarch

D0037118

Past Masters

AQUINAS Anthony Kenny
ARISTOTLE Jonathan Barnes
BACH Denis Arnold
FRANCIS BACON Anthony Quinton
BAYLE Elisabeth Labrousse
BERKELEY J. O. Urmson
THE BUDDHA Michael Carrithers
BURKE C. B. Macpherson
CARLYLE A. L. Le Quesne
CHAUCER George Kane
CLAUSEWITZ Michael Howard
COBBETT Raymond Williams
COLERIDGE Richard Holmes
CONFUCIUS Raymond Dawson
DANTE George Holmes
DARWIN Jonathan Howard
DIDEROT Peter France
GEORGE ELIOT Rosemary Ashton
GOETHE T. J. Reed
ENGELS Terrell Carver
GALILEO Stillman Drake

GOETHE T. J. Reed
HEGEL Peter Singer
HOMER Jasper Griffin
HUME A. J. Ayer
JESUS Humphrey Carpenter
KANT Roger Scruton
LAMARCK L. J. Jordanova
LEIBNIZ G. MacDonald Ross
LOCKE John Dunn
MACHIAVELLI Quentin Skinner
MARX Peter Singer
MENDEL Vitezslav Orel
MONTAIGNE Peter Burke
THOMAS MORE Anthony Kenny
WILLIAM MORRIS Peter Stansky
MUHAMMAD Michael Cook
NEWMAN Owen Chadwick
PASCAL Alban Krailsheimer
PETRARCH Nicholas Mann
PLATO R. M. Hare
PROUST Derwent May
TOLSTOY Henry Gifford

Forthcoming

AUGUSTINE Henry Chadwick
BERGSON Leszek Kolakowski
JOSEPH BUTLER R. G. Frey
CERVANTES P. E. Russell
COPERNICUS Owen Gingerich
DESCARTES Tom Sorell
DISRAELI John Vincent
ERASMUS James McConica
GIBBON J. W. Burrow
GODWIN Alan Ryan
HERZEN Aileen Kelly
JEFFERSON Jack P. Greene
JOHNSON Pat Rogers
KIERKEGAARD Patrick Gardiner
LEONARDO E. H. Gombrich

LINNAEUS W. T. Stearn
MILL William Thomas
NEWTON P. M. Rattansi
ST PAUL G. B. Caird
ROUSSEAU Robert Wokler
RUSKIN George P. Landow
RUSSELL John G. Slater
SHAKESPEARE Germaine Greer
ADAM SMITH D. D. Raphael
SOCRATES Bernard Williams
SPINOZA Roger Scruton
VICO Peter Burke
VIRGIL Jasper Griffin
WYCLIF Anthony Kenny

and others

Nicholas Mann

Petrarch

Oxford   New York

OXFORD UNIVERSITY PRESS

1984

Oxford University Press, Walton Street, Oxford OX2 6DP

London New York Toronto
Delhi Bombay Calcutta Madras Karachi
Kuala Lumpur Singapore Hong Kong Tokyo
Nairobi Dar es Salaam Cape Town
Melbourne Auckland

and associated companies in
Beirut Berlin Ibadan Mexico City Nicosia

Oxford is a trade mark of Oxford University Press

British Library Cataloguing in Publication Data

Mann, Nicholas
Petrarch.—(Past masters)
1. Petrarca, Francesco—Criticism and
interpretation
I. Title   II. Series
851'.1   PQ4540
ISBN 0–19–287610–4
ISBN 0–19–287609–0 Pbk

Library of Congress Cataloging in Publication Data

Mann, Nicholas.
Petrarch.
(Past masters)
Bibliography: p.
Includes index.
1. Petrarca, Francesco, 1304–1374—Criticism and
interpretation.   I. Title.   II. Series.
PQ4540.M3 1984   851'.1   84–4404
ISBN 0–19–287610–4
ISBN 0–19–287609–0 (pbk.)

Set by Hope Services, Abingdon
Printed in Great Britain by
Cox & Wyman Ltd, Reading

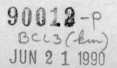

Contents

For Robert Bolgar
optimo praeceptori

1 The life as journey

Five figures in a landscape, classically clad: in the foreground, a shepherd seated and a farmer standing; behind them, a soldier, and a scholar drawing back a curtain to reveal a laurel-wreathed poet, reclining beneath a tree, pen in hand. This idyllic scene, the frontispiece of a manuscript containing the works of the Roman poet Virgil, depicts the fourth-century commentator Servius unveiling the mysteries of Virgil's three great poems, the *Aeneid*, the *Georgics* and the *Eclogues*, represented by their traditional protagonists—soldier, farmer and shepherd—carefully placed in descending order of social and literary hierarchy.

Three couplets of Latin verse, written in his own hand by Francesco Petrarca (who will henceforth be referred to by the English form of his name, Petrarch), explain the meaning of the miniature, which was executed at his behest around 1340 by the foremost exponent of the new Siennese style of painting, Simone Martini. The manuscript which it illuminates (now in the Ambrosian Library in Milan) was one whose copying Petrarch had supervised for his father, and which had been stolen shortly after its completion in 1326, only to be recovered some twelve years later. By that time, in his mid-thirties, Petrarch had already embarked upon a literary career that was to owe much to Virgil, and was a familiar figure at the papal court at Avignon, where Simone had come in 1336. It is as if, in celebrating the return of the manuscript by commissioning this modern, but classically inspired, illustration, he was marking his affection for it and its importance to him.

For the frontispiece to the Ambrosian Virgil holds within it in miniature many of the aspects of Petrarch's life and achievement with which this brief introduction will be concerned. As Servius unveils Virgil's poetry (and in the manuscript his commentary is, as was usual, written in the margins surrounding the text to which it applies), so, continuing the classical tradition, Petrarch unveils both text and commentary, adding his own erudite remarks on them in the outermost margins of each page. But his relationship with classical poetry, and Virgil's in particular, was not confined to the composition of such scholarly annotations, for he was to continue the classical tradition in a much less marginal way, writing works in imitation of Virgil—an epic poem called the *Africa*, twelve eclogues called the *Bucolicum Carmen* (Bucolic Song)—and of many other writers of ancient Rome, constantly having recourse to them for subject-matter and for style, attempting to return by emulation to a Latin which was purer and more correct than that commonly written in his day.

Indeed we might even take the reclining poet in the miniature for Petrarch rather than for Virgil, for the laurel wreath on his head reminds us of what is nowadays Petrarch's best-known claim to fame: his status as poet laureate, and his passion for a lady appropriately named Laura, expressed in a long sequence of Italian lyrics. It is perhaps no accident that on the flyleaf of the Virgil manuscript we find Petrarch's own laconic and possibly fictitious account of their meeting, in Avignon on 6 April 1327, and of her death, exactly twenty-one years later, as we also find a series of personal notes recording the deaths of other friends.

Such intimate annotations, spanning the whole of his career, mark the extent to which life and literature are interwoven: the classical text is not merely bounded by the signs of the scholar—annotation, exegesis and cross-reference—but prefaced by proofs of real friendship and an eminently literary love.

Finally, the frontispiece to the Ambrosian Virgil mirrors for us a further aspect of Petrarch's personality. It reflects the taste of the connoisseur of contemporary painting who, if we are to believe him, also owned, and probably commissioned, another significant picture. In two of his sonnets (C 77–8), he thanks Simone Martini for a portrait of Laura which revealed her divine beauty. Yet the connoisseur is also a moralist, for in his *Secretum* (Secret), a fictitious dialogue between himself and St Augustine, the character Augustinus reproaches Franciscus for seeking to make eternal in painted form the mortal face which had already caused him sufficient woes (SEC III 156). It is consonant with such characteristic moral reflection upon his love that later in life Petrarch was to own only a Madonna by Giotto, whose work he had always admired: the Virgin's image had finally supplanted that of the earthly love. Meanwhile, however, the Virgil manuscript marks an encounter more remarkable than that between a great love-poet and his lady. It embodies the meeting of two Italians of considerable stature, the foremost modern scholar who prepared the copy, and the foremost modern painter who illuminated it. And that meeting, like the meeting with Laura, took place in Avignon.

'Where the Pope is, there is Rome', as medieval doctrine had it: in the fourteenth century, all roads led to Avignon, where the papacy established itself for a period closely corresponding to the seventy-year span of

Petrarch's life (1304–74), bringing with it an enormous influx of Italians; Avignon became the centre of power, patronage and diplomacy. Petrarch's father, a Florentine notary by the name of Petracco, had been exiled from his native city only a few months after Dante in 1302, both men, conservatives, having fallen victim to a shift of power in favour of the radicals. After some years in Arezzo, where Petrarch and his brother Gherardo, three years his junior, were born, Petracco moved first to Pisa, and then, doubtless drawn by the openings which Avignon offered to a lawyer, to Carpentras, where the boys grew up within a few hours' ride of the papal court. As young men, they were often there; there it was that Petrarch found his first patron, and he was to spend the first fifteen years of his adult life either there, or at Vaucluse nearby.

Simone Martini, on the other hand, was one of a number of Italian artists brought to Avignon by Pope Benedict XII in the second half of the 1330s to carry out important commissions still visible today: religious frescos in the church of Notre-Dame des Doms, and wall-paintings in the papal palace full of natural detail, marking a turning-point in the history of art, the birth of the style known as the International Gothic.

For three-quarters of a century, Avignon was effectively the centre of the medieval world. Ideally situated geographically at the point where the major routes from Spain to Italy crossed the Rhone, strategically placed for political and diplomatic purposes, secure from the turmoil which afflicted Rome, it was a melting-pot of cultures and creeds, a crucible of learning, a sink of iniquity (as Petrarch repeatedly tells us), and a great magnet for men. To Avignon he owed not merely patronage and diplomatic employment, but endless encounters with people and with books, not least in the papal library, whose increasing stock of classical texts over the period of its expansion may to some degree reflect the influence of his tastes (even though the future Pope Innocent VI accused him of being a necromancer because he read Virgil!). From Avignon he was, however, eventually to escape, having come to detest what he calls the New Babylon, first to the rural solitude of his little house at the source of the Sorgue, at Vaucluse a few miles away, and finally to his beloved native Italy.

Yet despite the importance that it was to have in the first half of his life, Avignon was in one sense less of a meeting-place for Petrarch than a point of departure, for it is in his time there that we see developing one of the most characteristic features of his mature years: a constant restlessness and urge to travel. This trait, of which Petrarch was fully aware (he called himself *peregrinus ubique*: a wanderer, or pilgrim, everywhere) was to structure his daily life by imposing constant patterns of movement upon it, while also reflecting a profound aspect of his psychology: something between curiosity, the quest for the new, and a deep dissatisfaction, an unwillingness to settle down and define himself and his deepest concerns.

The more notable of his journeys away from Avignon can be swiftly charted: a summer's expedition to Lombez, the Pyrenees and Toulouse in 1330, a journey north across the Ardennes and to Cologne beyond in 1333, taking in Paris on the way, a remarkable excursion to the summit of Mont Ventoux in 1336, and visits to Rome in 1337, and 1341, when he travelled to Naples first. It was on his return from the last of these journeys, newly crowned poet laureate, that he decided to move his domicile to Parma; yet the pattern of movement which had been established was maintained, and he was to oscillate between Italy and Provence for another decade, going also to Naples again in 1343, and visiting many other Italian cities: Verona in 1345, Rome again and Genoa in 1350, Vicenza and Ferrara in 1351. Nor were his travels confined to Italy: during the eight years which he spent in Milan (from 1353 to 1361) he visited Basle and Prague in 1356 and Paris in 1360–1, and even the last twelve years of his life were divided between Venice and Pavia, Padua and finally Arquà, in the Euganean hills a few miles to the south, where he died on 18 July 1374 in the little house he had built himself there, two days before attaining his seventieth birthday. It is symptomatic of Petrarch's consciousness of this restlessness that in his will, drawn up in 1370, he should make provision for his burial in any one of seven places where death might strike him (T 6): to the last he saw himself as a traveller.

If we step back from the details of these movements, we can discern certain consistent motives and concerns. A good number of Petrarch's journeys were undertaken in the course of business (and indeed in later life he often regrets the time spent on such occasions): diplomatic missions in the interests of peace, or on behalf of patrons or powerful friends, such as those which took him to the French King Jean le Bon in Paris or the Emperor Charles IV in Prague. Others, however, were dictated by more personal affairs: in 1341 he went to Naples and Rome in pursuit of his greatest ambition, to be crowned with laurels, and again to Rome in the Jubilee Year of 1350, in a spirit of discovery and pilgrimage. Sometimes invitations drew him; on other occasions we know of no cause but curiosity and the thirst for knowledge, but we can at least measure the effects. For his travels brought him into contact with almost all the interlocking cultures of medieval Europe, with their rulers and statesmen, their monuments, and their books; he went, as he said, to return more learned, whether to the great university cities such as Paris or Padua, to that semi-deserted witness to antiquity that was Rome, or to the sites sung of by Virgil in the bay of Naples; and wherever he went, he sought out books which he bought or copied for his own library. It is no exaggeration to say that he owed many of his friendships, and some of his greatest intellectual discoveries, to his travels.

Once again, life and literature become indissolubly linked, and although Petrarch changes his view of voyages almost as often as he changes places, certain typical features emerge. First, the journey as a form of imitation, making his life conform to that of great men of the past, the Apostles, the Homeric heroes, and even St Augustine; second, journeys as an expression of dissatisfaction and the flight from men. But then, as we move deeper into his poetic fictions and as he nears the final harbour, he embarks more and more frequently upon the well-known classical image of life as a sea-voyage; that journey which had been represented as a pilgrimage for love becomes a flight from it, and from all the woes, spiritual and psychological, which it entails. At the same time, however, the realities of his travels continue to assert themselves: the tedium of official missions, the dangers of the road, the marvels of Rome, the natural beauties of Vaucluse, the Ardennes, the Apennines. The fusion of life, scholarship and literature is evident, for instance, in his *Itinerarium ad sepulcrum domini nostri Jesu Cristi* (Journey to the Tomb of Our Lord Jesus Christ), a guide-book on the pilgrimage to the Holy Land which he wrote without himself ever having undertaken the journey; and in a late letter (s IX 2) he even speaks of his study as a world of imaginary voyages, where reading or writing enable him to range over huge distances without exhaustion or loss of time.

Perhaps the clearest instance of such interplay between the real and the imagined is Petrarch's account, to which we shall have occasion to return, of his ascent of Mont Ventoux, some forty miles north-east of Avignon, in 1336. What purports to be a vivid description in the form of a letter written immediately after the climb (F IV 1) has been shown to be a carefully constructed allegory: his urge to reach the summit was not so much the single-minded ambition of the mountaineer as the painful aspiration of a man in search of spiritual heights. Climbing, like travelling, frequently recurs in his work as an image of man's condition; in the awareness which it betrays of the essential flux of human life, and the perpetual motion not only of the body but of the mind and the emotions, it is peculiarly Petrarchan, and, whilst owing much of its literary expression to the writers of antiquity, peculiarly modern. Petrarch's restlessness, and the fictions or poetic forms in which he so often explored it, are the signs of a man both aware of his potential and indeed of his achievement, and yet pro-foundly dissatisfied with them, a climber who reproaches himself with taking the easier downhill paths, a man modern in his self-consciousness yet medieval in his self-abasement, a man especially difficult to define because of the paradoxical fluctuations of his tempera-ment.

His travels across Europe reveal the man of letters as much in the role of enquirer as of that of ambassador, illustrating his passion for new places and his desire to know the sites of antiquity, his quest for knowledge and the books which would bring it, his pursuit of deeply held ideals such as peace and the idea of an Italy made new in the image of ancient Rome, and finally his alienation from a world which he saw as ever deteriorating, and from which he would frequently retire into solitude. His residence at Avignon made such travels, and his involvement in a life of action, possible and at times obligatory, yet also made possible the cultural achievement symbolised by Simone Martini's frontispiece to his Virgil manuscript, and paradoxically even opened up to Petrarch the path to the life of contemplation which he professed to prefer. It will be a constant theme of this book that the images are as important as the supposed realities: that Petrarch's self-awareness obliges us to consider what we know of the everyday details of his life (and we know a great deal, for he was careful to document it) as part of a complex literary structure in which reality and fiction are inextricably intertwined.

2 The life of the intellect

Surveying his childhood with the knowing detachment of old age, Petrarch singles out as one of the earliest events of any significance in his life the burning of some of his favourite books by his father. But then books play a crucial role in his perception of his own development, and must occupy a leading position in any account of him. Not only did he spend a great deal of time searching for them, reading them and working on them (as well as writing them), but he treated them, as the Virgil manuscript reveals, as confidants and close companions, dear friends with whom he was constantly in conversation, both the sources of and the witnesses to his intellectual progress. If, more than half a century after the event, he thus should choose to recall, for the benefit of a correspondent and ultimately for that of posterity (s XVI 1), that when he was fifteen his father, catching him reading classical literature instead of studying law, had burned all his books but two—works by Virgil and Cicero—it is surely not fortuitous, for the whole of his subsequent career is a triumphant demonstration of the futility of that act of paternal repression.

The present chapter will be more concerned with the making than with the destruction of Petrarch's books, but also with what he made of those that he read. The story of his lifelong relationship with them can in part be verified from the substantial number of manuscripts from his collection which survive today. But inevitably much of it rests solely upon his carefully considered accounts, often written many years after the event and showing every sign of hindsight and deliberate arrangement. Even the urge to embellish the facts with the fictions of the self-aware, however, is an important feature both of Petrarch's consciousness of his intellectual identity, and of his cultural significance as emergent man of letters.

Petrarch's first formal education came from an obscure schoolmaster named Convenevole da Prato, who instilled in him the elements of grammar and rhetoric while he was living at Carpentras. Yet even at this early stage, when other children were reading Aesop's fables, he was, he tells us, already instinctively drawn to the works of Cicero, scarcely understanding them but captivated by the sweetness and sonority of the words (s xvi 1). By the time that he was twelve, however, his father had decided that he should follow in his footsteps and study Law. He accordingly sent him to the University of Montpellier, which evidently did little to dampen his enthusiasm for classical literature (since it is from this period that the book-burning incident dates), and doubtless also brought him into contact with the vernacular love-poetry of Provence.

In the autumn of 1320 Petrarch and his brother Gherardo and a young friend called Guido Sette were sent to the greatest centre of legal learning in medieval Europe, the University of Bologna, where they remained, with interruptions, until the spring of 1326. Yet Petrarch's legal studies seem never fully to have engaged his attention or interest; he admits to having spent his time there too on literature. Besides, Bologna was an important intellectual centre, where he met many of his future friends, and encountered for the first time that Italian vernacular lyric poetry to which he was to make such a decisive contribution. Ironically, his studies there signalled the end of his legal career, but these were formative years which gave him an excellent grounding in classical literature. The major figures of his late adolescence, Virgil and Cicero and, as we shall see, St Augustine, were to remain with him for the whole of his life.

From 1326 onwards, Petrarch seems to have been firmly launched upon a literary career, supported initially by his father and then by ecclesiastical benefices and the generosity of patrons. What was fast becoming a passion for books was readily fuelled by the papal library and a flourishing book trade in Avignon, and it was there, while still in his twenties, that he accomplished his first significant piece of literary research, to which we shall return in the next chapter: the reconstruction of Livy's *Roman History*. But his travels too had a part to play, and his journey to the north in 1333, for instance, yielded exceptional fruit in the shape of a hitherto unknown oration (*Pro Archia*) by Cicero, found at Liège, and the writings of the Roman elegiac poet Propertius, discovered in Paris. The result was that by the beginning of his thirties, and before his first visit to Rome, he had already amassed a significant collection of books with a marked preference for the philosophy, poetry and history of antiquity.

The pattern thus established was to continue until the end of Petrarch's life, and his library to grow to be the largest private collection of classical literature in existence in his day. Perhaps his most significant discovery was that of a manuscript of Cicero's *Letters to Atticus* at Verona in 1345, but there are dozens of other instances of his finding, receiving or acquiring classical texts, and evidence of his studying them. A catalogue would be wearisome, but there is no doubt that at least until his sixty-fifth year, when he had the Latin translation of Homer's works copied, he was constantly searching for, and reading, the great works of the past.

Looking back in his mid-fifties, Petrarch speaks of Cicero and Virgil as almost a father and a brother, experiencing for them an affection greater than for any living man (F XXII 10). Cicero ('my Cicero', as he frequently calls him) was constantly by his side, and, as we shall see, in his writings. The letters which he found in 1345 were to become the model for his own, two of which (F XXIV 3–4) he actually addressed to Cicero; in 1359 he even reproaches the Roman writer for hurting him, telling how one day as he was entering his library his clothes caught in his copy of the Letters, a huge volume, and brought it down on his left leg, bruising him badly. 'I picked the book up with a smile and said: "Why, my dear Cicero, why do you wound me so?" No answer came, yet again the following day he hurt me when I returned' (F XXI 10). And one of the last letters that Petrarch ever wrote, the one in which he relates the burning of his books, is almost entirely devoted to Cicero.

This filial affection for the great Roman writer, not untempered by criticism, but almost unlimited in its intellectual impact, was a trait which Petrarch shared with St Augustine, who was undoubtedly his favourite Christian writer, and was more than any other responsible for a shift in his later years away from pagan literature to the Church Fathers. Indeed Petrarch's identification with St Augustine was even more intense than with Cicero. He saw him as the most profound influence upon his spiritual and intellectual development, and even went so far as to cast him in the *Secretum* in the role not so much of father confessor as of *alter ego*: himself as he felt he ought to be.

From his first recorded book purchase, a copy of the *City of God*, at Avignon in 1325, and perhaps from even earlier, his reading of the saint's writings was constant: four of them figure as virtually the only non-classical texts among his favourite books around 1333; it was in that year that he was given a copy of Augustine's *Confessions*, a work which was profoundly to influence his outlook on the world and himself, and to travel with him until the end of his life. Just as Augustine was led to the truth by Cicero, so Petrarch, guided by Augustine, sought out the Roman writer; just as Augustine turned from temporal concerns and classical literature to the spiritual life and works of piety, so too Petrarch attempted to reform his own life, and consciously to restructure it for posterity.

Living men too had an important role to play in shaping Petrarch's culture. His brother Gherardo, who became a Carthusian monk, and his closest friends, such as his childhood companion Guido Sette (later Archdeacon of Genoa), or the Roman Lello di Pietro Stefano dei Tosetti (whom Petrarch calls Lelius in his letters) or the Flemish musician Ludwig van Kempen (called Socrates), or the Augustinian theologian Dionigi da Borgo San Sepolcro (who gave him the *Confessions*), or Philippe de Cabassoles, bishop of Cavaillon and later cardinal and papal legate, were all responsible in different ways for significant aspects of his development. So too were Florentine admirers encountered much later in life such as the prior Francesco Nelli, the jurist Lapo da Castiglionchio, or the fellow-humanist and writer Giovanni Boccaccio. The same is equally true of certain of his patrons and protectors: bishop Giacomo Colonna and his brother the cardinal Giovanni, to whose household Petrarch was attached for some seventeen years from 1330 onwards, or Azzo da Correggio, sometime ruler of Parma, or the Visconti under whose protection he lived for eight years in Milan, and on whose behalf he undertook several important diplomatic missions, or the patrons of his later years, notably Andrea Dandolo, Doge of Venice, and the rulers of Padua, Iacopo da Carrara and his son Francesco. Nor should we ignore the influence of King Robert of Sicily, to whom in part Petrarch owed his coronation, and of other major statesmen such as Pope Urban V or the Emperor Charles IV.

Yet in approaching the question of his relations with living men, whether they be servants and unknown correspondents or the most powerful figures of the medieval world, we are obliged to have recourse to the same kind of evidence as bears on his relations with those long dead: what he wrote about them. Indeed the principal, and frequently the only source of our knowledge of Petrarch's friendships is his correspondence, which is resolutely literary in conception, content and expression. It must also have been voluminous, for he claims to have destroyed at least a thousand letters (F I I), and eighty of those addressed to him have survived. At all events, he carefully preserved and edited some six hundred of his letters for posterity. None of these is trivial: even those which appear to deal with insignificant matters are never less than exercises in style and rhetorical formulation, while many of the major epistles are in effect set pieces: essays in consolation or exhortation, or small treatises on topics of general interest such as politics, government, education, philosophy, illness and death. Many, too, take as their pretext the composition, or sending, or receiving or requesting of letters or books, and thus tell us as much about the problems of writing as about the nature of personal relations. So that in considering the influences upon Petrarch's intellectual development we cannot ignore his correspondence, and this in turn obliges us to take into account both the self-consciousness of his writing, and his awareness of all its implications for the image of himself that he was seeking to establish.

But it is above all the impact of Petrarch's reading which is significant. From the very beginning of his career as writer, the formative influence of classical models is evident. His research on Livy during the 1320s inspired him to compose his own work of Roman history, the *De viris illustribus* (On Famous Men), which he began at Vaucluse in 1337. The starting-point was a life of Scipio Africanus, a figure to whom he was particularly attached, but he gradually added other lives to it, and by 1343 had composed a series of twenty-three biographical portraits of great Romans, arranged chronologically from Romulus to Cato the Censor; the work of expansion and rewriting was to continue sporadically until the end of his days. A year after beginning the *De viris illustribus*, he started on what was intended as its poetic counterpart, an epic with Scipio as hero, accordingly named *Africa*, and apparently conceived of at Vaucluse in Holy Week 1333. The literary model here was Virgil's *Aeneid*; the principal material sources were Livy, Eusebius and other historians, Cicero's *Dream of Scipio*, and Petrarch's own observations among the ruins of Rome.

In 1343, still at Vaucluse, Petrarch began another work of classical history, the *Rerum memorandarum libri* (Books of Memorable Matters), this time inspired by the *Memorabilia* of the Roman writer Valerius Maximus, a series of *exempla*: the words and deeds of the great men of the past, gathered and authenticated with all the authority of his scholarly researches in Livy and elsewhere. And in 1346, yet again in Vaucluse, he returned once more to Virgil, whose *Eclogues* gave birth to a series of purportedly pastoral poems later to evolve into the *Bucolicum carmen*.

Perhaps the most influential of all his Roman models, however, was Cicero. Petrarch's discovery of his letters at Verona in 1345 led him subsequently to model his own correspondence upon them, conceiving of letters already written and yet to be written as forming first one collection (*Rerum familiarium libri*: 350 prose letters on 'familiar matters' in twenty-four books, ten of those in the final book being addressed to great writers of antiquity), then a second (*Rerum senilium libri*: 127 letters written in later life arranged in eighteen books, the final one of which was to consist of a single *Letter to Posterity*). And finally the major achievement of Petrarch's maturity, his moral encyclopedia *De remediis utriusque fortune* (Remedies for Both Kinds of Fortune) completed in 1366, owes the structure of its dialogues to Cicero's *Tusculan Disputations*, and rather more than five hundred of the exemplary figures whom it quotes to the history and literature of antiquity.

The only non-classical author to have had such a profound impact upon the shaping of Petrarch's writings was St Augustine, himself as we have already seen steeped in the classics; his *Confessions* were the inspiration and latent model for the *Secretum*, composed between 1347 and 1353. Yet the influence of the past upon Petrarch was not confined to matters of structure or literary form: it extends to the very substance of his works. In the case of the *Africa*, *De viris illustribus* and

Rerum memorandarum libri, where the subject-matter is itself predominantly classical, this is hardly surprising. Nor, given the Ciceronian antecedent, is the increasing use of classical quotation and reference in his correspondence particularly unexpected, though it is important to remember that much of it is related to everyday matters, revealing the extent to which the writers of antiquity were alive in Petrarch's consciousness.

More striking, however, is the fundamental and powerful presence of classical poetry in his Italian lyrics, and the constant recourse to classical (and therefore pagan) quotations or references in the more explicitly religious of his Latin writings, reflecting the evident influence of the writers of antiquity upon his spiritual development. The case of Cicero is exemplary: he is frequently quoted (often on St Augustine's authority) in Petrarch's treatises on the solitary life (*De vita solitaria*, begun in 1346 but not completed until many years later) and on monastic tranquillity (*De otio religioso*, mainly composed in 1346 after a visit to Gherardo in the Charterhouse of Montrieux); Ciceronian psychological and moral attitudes are much echoed, and explicitly debated, in the *Secretum*. And even Petrarch's last major work, the *De sui ipsius et aliorum ignorantia* (On His Own Ignorance and That of Others), begun in 1367, is profoundly indebted to Cicero.

But the debt is even greater than this concern with form or content might suggest. Addressing in 1359 to Boccaccio what is more of a manifesto on literary imitation than a letter, Petrarch speaks of the way in which the works of his favourite authors had impressed themselves not merely upon his memory, but upon the very marrow of his being, rooting themselves deeply in the innermost recesses of his mind, leading him to forget who wrote them, and even that anyone else had written them (F XXII 2). This intense intellectual absorption of his sources, this taking possession of other men's writings and transmuting them into his own, is a characteristic feature of Petrarch's literary genius, as is the awareness which accompanies it. His theoretical position, delineated in a number of the *Familiares*, is that the process of imitation should not be a servile one of copying and borrowing, but a creative one of remoulding and remaking, evoked in the classical image of bees turning the nectar they ingest into wax and honey (F I 8). His aim is to achieve similarity of style and vision without indulging in identity of expression (F XXII 2); the imitator should 'take care that what he writes resembles the original without reproducing it precisely. The resemblance should not be that of a portrait to the sitter . . . but of a son to his father, where there is often a great divergence in particular features, and yet a certain suggestion which makes the likeness: what painters call an "air", most noticeable about the face and eyes' (F XXIII 19).

There is ample evidence in Petrarch's writings of the intellectual processes involved: first, the initial reading of the work; second, the digestion of this reading: its absorption and modification by contrast with other reading; finally, the act of writing. These three activities form a perpetual cycle in Petrarch's literary life: he was for ever reading and rereading, reflecting and comparing, and, of course, writing. But there is a final stage, which has left its mark upon all his works: the further self-critical scrutiny to which every written word is submitted, as the conscious mind takes over and applies the theoretical criteria of imitation, eliminating anything which might seem too close to its model, and endlessly rewriting in search of perfection.

The dilemma behind this is one which is central to the classical tradition, and had been graphically summarised by a twelfth-century scholar, Bernard of Chartres, who had described his contemporaries as dwarfs on the shoulders of giants, able to see further than their predecessors, but only because they were raised up upon their colossal shoulders. The humanist (in the original sense of classical scholar) of the twelfth century, as indeed his fourteenth-century successor, was constantly aware of all that made his elevated position possible, yet also of the implications of that elevated position: he was uniquely placed to outshine his models. To progress beyond the tradition from which he had sprung is a fundamental Petrarchan aspiration, and his efforts to achieve this are a familiar topic in his writings. As the *De viris illustribus*, for instance, evolved away from Livy, its design became increasingly ambitious. Petrarch took it up again in the 1350s, rewriting the introduction and adding a new series of biographies stretching from Adam to Hercules; he expanded the life of Scipio to well over 10,000 words, and later drafted a monumental life of Julius Caesar which was to occupy him until his death. The material was classical, but the conception of the phenomenon of man which Petrarch imposed upon it was his alone.

Similarly, the *Rerum memorandarum libri* extended the historical schema suggested by Valerius Maximus to include non-Roman and even contemporary examples such as Dante and King Robert of Sicily. What might have been a simple collation of historical data became, within the framework of the four cardinal Christian virtues under whose heading the material was arranged, a real attempt to bring the past to life by investigating the motivation and psychology that lay behind the memorable facts and sayings which Petrarch had gathered.

The *Africa*, far from being merely an attempt (albeit unsuccessful) to emulate Virgil, was intended to enshrine all of Petrarch's scholarly accomplishments and to demonstrate his poetic talents. It was a powerful project, reflecting his very considerable erudition and his enthusiasm for ancient Rome and the Roman ideal. It combined the history of Scipio's epic struggle with allegorical descriptions, a love-story, and even a dream in which Homer appears to the classical poet Ennius (who had transmitted the glories of the Greek past) and tells him of the Latin poets of the future, and in particular of Petrarch and his *Africa*, posterity's sole witness to the glories of the Roman past.

The ambition to achieve fame through posterity, to be a latter-day Homer, is never far from the surface of Petrarch's works. In the *Bucolicum carmen*, for instance, he borrows the pastoral mode from Virgil to explore, as his model had done, a number of literary and political issues, using idyllic characters and rustic imagery to discuss the corruption of the papal court at Avignon, the return of the papacy to Rome, or the ravages of the plague which had swept Europe in 1348. Yet, significantly, the longest and most obscure of his twelve eclogues, and the one to which he devoted most attention, is the tenth, describing the death of the laurel. For this laurel is both Laura and classical poetry; its demise leaves the solitary Silvanus— Petrarch—to carry the torch of learning and literature into the future.

But imitation, whatever its aims, was not simply a matter of literary accomplishment. Just as we have seen that Cicero and Augustine, to name but two, were almost more real to Petrarch than many living men, so we may also perceive that his desire for emulation extended beyond books to the lives and achievements of great men of the past. In his younger days he had identified with his hero Scipio; his coronation in 1341 was consonant with this identification, and clearly conceived (as we shall see) in a spirit of classical imitation; as a love poet he even went so far on occasions as to compare himself with the sun-god Apollo, patron of music and poetry; later in life he toyed with the pleasing idea of dying in Mantua because Virgil was born there (v 24), or dying reading like Ptolemy (s 1 5), or dying writing like Plato (s xv 6). But it is indicative of the profound influence of St Augustine upon him that in his most intimate work, the *Secretum*, he reveals the extent to which he wished to interpret his own life, and transgressions, and reading, as parallel to those of the saint: the sinner, nourished on classical literature, who turns to God. At the same time, however, he retains the lucidity to observe that he had not yet succeeded in that ultimate act of emulation: at the end of the debate, Franciscus has not wholly been won over by Augustinus.

There is here, as in many of Petrarch's writings, a certain elusiveness, a sense of incompleteness. That this was a feature of his character, mirroring a deep inner dissatisfaction and an inability to put the finishing touches to any work, seems clear. It is as if the creative task, and the intellectual autobiography which grows from it, is perennially open-ended. The three great classicising enterprises of his early period of creativity, the *De viris illustribus*, *Africa* and *Rerum memorandarum libri*, occupied him sporadically until his death, and were never completed; the *Secretum*, set in 1342 but probably begun in 1347, was substantially revised in 1352–3; the *Bucolicum carmen* evolved slowly from 1346 onwards, but the fair copy which Petrarch made in 1357 was considerably amended over the course of the next nine years; the *De vita solitaria*, started in the same year as the eclogues, was not finally completed until 1371; the *De otio religioso*, first drafted in 1347, was not put into definitive form until ten years later. Even so late a work as the *De ignorantia*, first penned in 1367, underwent substantial revision, and the *Letter to Posterity*, several times reworked in the last fifteen years of Petrarch's life, was, not surprisingly, never brought to a conclusion.

What is true of works that were, broadly speaking, conceived of at a single moment and as single units is all the truer of those made up of large numbers of shorter pieces composed over a period of years; in particular, of the collections of letters, whether in prose (*Familiares*, *Seniles* and *Sine nomine*) or in verse (*Epistole*), and of Petrarch's vernacular poetry: the great cycle of 366 lyrics now usually known as the *Canzoniere* but which he called his *Rerum vulgarium fragmenta* (Vernacular Fragments), and the six *Trionfi* (Triumphs). No fewer than nine phases have been identified in the evolution of the *Canzoniere* (and further research may well reveal further subtleties) as Petrarch's conception gradually evolved: the earliest poems were written at the beginning of his twenties; the idea of forming them into a cycle first emerges in 1342; the elaboration of the final form of that cycle dates from the last two years of his life and even then was not, nor ever could be, truly complete. Similarly, the first of the *Trionfi*, the Triumph of Love, was conceived in the 1330s, apparently as an independent poem. The idea of a cycle, running through the Triumphs of Chastity, Death, Fame and Time, only emerges much later, and Petrarch was to continue to work on the poems until the year of his death, when he finally composed the Triumph of Eternity.

The *Familiares* provide a particularly graphic illustration of the evolutionary process, and of the difficulties it creates for the historian in search of a neat chronological schema with which to document Petrarch's intellectual development. He must have been keeping copies of his correspondence since the 1320s; only after discovering Cicero's letters in 1345, however, did the idea of editing his own letters into a collection apparently occur to him: at that stage it would seem that his project was to divide them into twelve books in imitation of the structure of the *Aeneid*. Later, in the early 1350s, he came to favour a twenty-book model based on Seneca's *Letters to Lucilius*, and finally settled, by 1360, for twenty-four books in imitation of Homer. Meanwhile, Petrarch had been assiduously gathering his letters and writing new ones. The 350 which he finally chose to transcribe in the definitive form of the *Familiares* completed in 1366 had been carefully selected, ordered and edited. Some, rhetorical set-pieces, had been written specially, others substantially rewritten, sometimes more than once, others still ascribed to fictitious dates. Many of the earlier letters, ostensibly dating back to the 1330s and 1340s, make considerable use of quotations from and references to classical texts not known to Petrarch until at least a decade later; attitudes and sentiments attributed to one part of his life are often the fruit of reflection, rewriting and editorial intervention by the older man, concerned to order and enhance the fragments of his experience.

The *Familiares* illustrate not merely the creative urge

to form a major work out of what might have otherwise remained minor fragments, but also an equally characteristic Petrarchan dissatisfaction (which in the later collection of *Seniles* becomes a frequent and explicit theme rather than, as here, an underlying inspiration for literary artifice): the sense that all his writing is eternally capable of correction and improvement. Indeed, Petrarch often speaks, following Horace among others, of filing and polishing his works, and habitually kept his friends informed by letter of alterations or additions that he had made to them. The surviving autograph manuscripts of both his Latin and his Italian writings carry copious evidence of the editorial process: erasures, marginal additions, notes to himself about desirable changes. And, interestingly, a certain amount of this evidence combines with the strategically preserved discussion of problems of writing in certain letters to illuminate the crucial humanist topic of imitation, singling out lines of verse where Petrarch had unconsciously followed a classical poet too closely for his liking, and where he self-consciously identifies his model, judges his imitation too servile, and amends it to his satisfaction (F XXII 2, XXIII 19). The same process can sometimes be detected in letters which survive in several redactions: a first in which a classical quotation is unidentified; a second in which it is ascribed to its source, and a definitive revision in which it is finally eliminated, to be replaced by some maxim of Petrarch's own making (F IV 2).

This literary and cultural self-consciousness defies orderly analysis. The constant implicit or explicit recourse to classical models, whether in the first conception of a written text or in some subsequent revision of it, and the frequent evidence of the desire to outdo those models, to forge a new and superior literary

25

identity transcending imitation, cannot readily be correlated with major moments in Petrarch's intellectual or
spiritual development, given the extended process of
composition through which all his works went, best
described as a state of creative flux lasting an indeter-
minate number of years. Yet it is a significant topos (and
a good Augustinian one) of Petrarch's maturity that at a
certain moment he turned his back on the classics and
directed his attention to sacred literature.

That we should not take the topos for the whole truth
is, however, clear from his own statements concerning
the impact of his reading of the classics upon his
memory, and from the evidence of his continued concern
with the authors of antiquity almost until his dying day:
one account has it that he died with Homer in his hands,
and he was certainly still working on his life of Caesar in
the last weeks of his life. But that he underwent a major
spiritual crisis in the 1340s is an important element of
his literary autobiography: we find it reflected in the
Secretum, many of the poems of the *Canzoniere*, the
Psalmi penitentiales (Penitential Psalms) which he
composed in 1343, and a number of his letters. It may
have been inspired by Gherardo's profession as a Carthusian monk in 1342, and seems to have evolved over the
succeeding decade. It did not suddenly convert Petrarch
from classical scholarship and poetry to scriptural and
patristic writings, but the function of the crisis, whether
real or literary, was to break the exclusive hold of the
classics on his attention and imagination, and to allow
him to devote more thought to spiritual questions. From
the 1350s onwards his erudition is more reflective: his
writings become increasingly concerned with death and
the proper Christian preparation for it. The shift is not
announced, however, until a letter probably written in
1360 (F XXII 10); in 1366, having reached the beginning of

his sixty-third year and thus the medieval grand climacteric, Petrarch looks back and carefully dates the fullness of his change of heart to 1350, the year of the Jubilee and his third visit to Rome (s VIII 1); the following year he ascribes to Augustine's *Confessions* his conversion to sacred literature (s VIII 6), an attribution already implicit in the *Secretum*, though there he also claims to have been converted by *On True Religion*, where Augustine admits his own debt to the classics; in the last year of his life he regrets the blind errors of his Cicero-hunting youth when he never used to touch the works of the Church Fathers (s XVI 1).

That the omnivorous admirer of classical antiquity, whose appetite for every aspect of the ancient world we shall have further occasion to investigate in the following chapter, should, as an older man perceiving the vanity of temporal things, insist upon his change of heart, even as he continues to reveal in his writings his deep attachment to the past, and to his own past, is entirely in accordance with Petrarch's self-awareness as author and his eternal state of spiritual flux. In the very letter in which he condemns his youth (s XVI 1), he boasts of being the first of his contemporaries to have restored the classical usage of the second person singular form of address, and in another, written to Boccaccio only a few months earlier, he asserts his authoritative role as the reviver of classical studies in Italy, and stresses the importance of not abandoning them (s XVII 2). As he prepares for death, paradoxically he persists in his personal myth of survival: the humanist scholar's mission to bring the fruits of his learning to the modern world. The dwarf who strove both to avail himself to the full of the gigantic literary edifice upon which he was sitting, and yet to develop a vision reaching beyond it, has finally become a giant.

3 The active and contemplative lives

One immediate consequence of Petrarch's devotion to the past was an intense dislike (whether theoretical or real, at least frequently made explicit) of the modern world. Yet it is a further paradox of his activities and intellectual attitudes that despite this he was deeply committed to certain urgent contemporary issues, and much involved in major fourteenth-century political questions. To this commitment he brought the full force of his considerable learning, while at the same time constantly lamenting his involvement and expressing his desire for escape to a more tranquil state which might leave him freer to pursue the studies of his predilection. When we look back on his achievement from the twentieth century, it is in part at least for his active and not his contemplative life that we admire him, as committed intellectual rather than as ivory-tower academic. The present chapter will explore the contradictions which arise from his scholarly pursuits.

'I am alive now yet I would rather have been born at some other time' (vs I 8); 'I never liked this present age' (p 6): these are characteristic Petrarchan disavowals of his own day, of a kind often coupled with scathing comments on the *vulgus*, ordinary people. The obvious escape was antiquity, and his writings abound with expressions of his love of the past and the men of the past. At the same time, as we have seen, those writings reflect not simply a literary contact, but a conscious emulation, whether in the form of identification with historical individuals such as Scipio or, later, Julius

Caesar, or by imitation of great writers such as Cicero or Virgil, or finally by the re-creation of antiquity through works such as the *Africa* or *De viris illustribus*, or even through actions such as his coronation. This emulation, together with an insatiable curiosity for all things classical (symbolised for instance by his attempts around 1342 to learn Greek, at a time when almost no one could read it), makes of Petrarch one of the founders of the Renaissance. The ancient civilisation which he was among the first systematically to explore and restore was to exercise a profound influence on every aspect of European culture from his day onwards, and is still with us today.

Apart from the reading already referred to in the previous chapter, the earliest evidence we have of his learned activities is a remarkable instance of textual scholarship which occupied him in his early twenties: the piecing together and reconstruction of the text of Livy's great history of Rome, begun *c.*25 BC and originally consisting of 142 books, divided into groups of ten known as decades. The work only survived in fragmentary form in the early fourteenth century; Petrarch started with an incomplete eleventh- or twelfth-century copy of the third decade, and in 1325 or 1326 added to it a copy of the first decade, part of which he transcribed in his own hand. Then, perhaps four years later, when he was in Avignon, Landolfo Colonna, a Canon of Chartres related to the family under whose patronage Petrarch was then living, brought him a manuscript of the fourth decade, until then completely forgotten. Petrarch identified it and united it with the first and third and thus, by the time he was twenty-five or twenty-six, had succeeded in putting together for himself the most complete text of Livy in existence in his day.

But he did not simply perform an elementary act of restoration, for his manuscript, which is preserved today in the British Library, is marked by the traces of an intense philological activity which make it in effect the first scholarly edition of the *Roman History*. Not content with the text as it stood, Petrarch drew on other manuscripts to amend the first decade and to correct and complete the third, annotating the text copiously on the basis of these other witnesses, and finally establishing the original outline of Livy's work, recognising Colonna's manuscript as the fourth decade lacking only a single book, and perceiving that his own copy was missing the second decade. This achievement he triumphantly announced to posterity in a letter addressed to Livy which he probably wrote much later, in 1350, and placed in the final book of his *Familiares* (F xxiv 8).

An erudite enterprise of this kind (of much greater complexity than such a summary suggests) was, whatever its limitations, of the highest significance for classical scholarship. A century later, Petrarch's manuscript was used to great advantage by one of the major classical scholars of the Renaissance, Lorenzo Valla; it remained the fullest text of Livy available for two centuries; six and a half centuries on, Petrarch's annotations and emendations are still of value and interest to contemporary scholars. His work on Livy may stand as an exemplary instance of the kind of pioneering philological activity which he inaugurated, and of his pivotal role between the great writers of antiquity and the modern world to which he bequeathed them. We owe a great deal of our knowledge of classical authors today—notably of Cicero, but also of such others as the poet Propertius or the geographer Pomponius Mela—to Petrarch's research, discoveries and textual work.

He was not, however, simply a textual critic, though his urge to establish the correct text, revealed by his earliest achievement, the preparation of his father's Virgil manuscript, was clearly a compelling one. He was also in the fullest sense a scholar, deeply immersed in the world which he so preferred to his own age, a reader whose annotations reveal both what was for the fourteenth century an extraordinary breadth of classical learning, and a remarkable acuity of critical intelligence. The annotations in the Ambrosian Virgil, made from the time of its recovery in 1338 onwards, are clear evidence of this: there are hundreds of marginal notes and glosses, drawing on more than forty different classical writers (not to mention medieval ones) and constituting a formidable network of cross-references which demonstrate the range of Petrarch's reading, his agility in handling his sources, and his determination to elucidate both Virgil's text and Servius's commentary upon it.

It has also to be admitted, however, that his interest, and his critical talents, lay in the purely scholarly domain: the identification of technical aspects of classical style and prosody, the establishment of the literal meaning of an accurate text, and the recognition of literary devices and references. Petrarch was not, in our terms, an exciting or innovative literary critic, but adopted the traditional medieval interpretation of the *Aeneid*, seeking for the moral truths concealed behind the allegorical veil of poetic fiction (s IV 5). He may have been aware that such a process was not unexceptionable, for he allows Augustinus in the *Secretum* to reproach Franciscus for precisely such a reading (SEC II 124), but his true interest was that of the historian: a burning desire for an accurate account of the facts of the past. Thus he constantly juxtaposes with Servius's comments quotations from or references to classical historians; he draws equally on the poets when he can. His aim, as he emphasises elsewhere, and notably in the preface to the *De viris illustribus*, is to retell history as it really was rather than simply to retail the fables of the past, and this he hopes to achieve by the critical evaluation and comparison of sources, and the identification of significant detail. Thus his probing mind seizes upon the love of Dido and Aeneas in Virgil's great poem, and demonstrates that it was historically impossible, since Dido was born some 300 years after Aeneas's death. His denunciation of the myth was a matter of some satisfaction to him, and in a letter written in his early sixties he claims to be the only man of his generation to have revealed its falsehood, quoting Roman and patristic sources for his certainty, and vaunting his knowledge of chronology and history (s iv 5).

There is something mildly paradoxical about the historian's triumph over the poet's fiction in this case, for Petrarch's vernacular poetry is suffused with the very myth of romantic love that he is in this case at such pains to dissipate. But there is no doubt that in his Latin writings his historical interests are overriding. The focus of his attention was Rome, and it is symptomatic that he should for instance have heavily annotated his manuscript of the Latin translation of Eusebius's *Chronicon*, correcting and querying dates and the precise sequence of events, and even commenting, on the basis of his personal observations, on the dating of some of the major monuments of ancient Rome. That he could thus challenge an authority of such standing shows the confidence that Petrarch had in the value of his own scholarship, and that he should concern himself with buildings, rightly declaring the Pantheon not to be

contemporary with the Capitol, reveals another important aspect of his concern with antiquity: his passion for
all its tangible remains.

When he first travelled to Rome in 1337, he spent some
time visiting its sites with another member of the
Colonna family, a Dominican historian named Giovanni.
The account which he subsequently composed is somewhat bookish, mentioning the monuments in their
historical order rather than that in which he saw them
(F VI 2), and may indeed owe more to one or another of
the unreliable medieval guide-books to the city than to
any acute personal observation: he moves chronologically
through the history of Rome from its mythical beginnings in Evander's dwelling-place down to the age of the
Christian martyrs, trying to identify ruins often so
dilapidated and overgrown as to be unrecognisable,
evoking past glories rather than the fragmented realities
of the present. There is here a curious mixture of
genuine scholarly research (he corrected a number of
traditional errors, and challenged Colonna on the strength
of his reading of Eusebius), of failure to observe (he
attributed the Ponte Sant'Angelo to Trajan, despite the
fact that Hadrian's name was very clearly inscribed on
both sides of it), and deliberate mythologising (which
was to bear its most striking fruit in a poetic evocation of
the topography of ancient Rome in the eighth book of the
Africa). But the enthusiasm behind it is evident, and
characteristic of Petrarch's scholarship.

Not only his properly historical works (*De viris
illustribus, Rerum memorandarum libri*), but also all
his Latin writings and his Italian lyrics bear the evidence
of his deep concern for antiquity, ranging from the
calculation of dates and correction of false attributions,
or the identification of classical borrowings in patristic

authors, to the discussion and imitation of classical texts, and the ubiquitous recourse to examples and quotations from them. Petrarch's philology is as total an involvement with the past as was possible in his day.

Thus he read Vitruvius's treatise on architecture (which was to have a profound influence upon Renaissance building), and studied ancient maps so as to establish the facts; he even collected coins to further his understanding of Roman history, referring to them as evidence for the wilful features of the Emperor Vespasian (RM II 73), or using them to unravel obscure passages in the historians, or as visual aids to persuade the Emperor Charles IV of the examples that he should follow (F XIX 3). Indeed, in 1361 Charles actually called him in as an expert to evaluate two documents claimed by Rudolf IV of Austria to be privileges granted by Julius Caesar and Nero, and justifying Austria's independence within the Empire. Petrarch's triumphant demonstration of the inauthenticity of these documents on stylistic, terminological and historical grounds (S XVI 5) is a fine instance both of the quality of his scholarship and of the way in which he was able to use it for the purposes of contemporary affairs: the scholar is not simply a self-indulgent academic delighting in the vanished world of the past, but a pundit and adviser to great men, vitally involved in the active life of the present.

For, as Augustinus reminds Franciscus (SEC III 162), the lessons of reading must be applied. Moreover it is almost an article of faith for Petrarch that the historian has a duty to his contemporaries (and even, as we shall see in later chapters, to posterity), that it is not sufficient merely to enjoy knowledge of the past: it must be put to good use. The great men of classical times will provide examples of right action, and a great civilisation a model for the present (or, in its passing, an instance of the futility of human endeavour, for the Christian moralist can often override the humanist scholar, and the familiar medieval topos of *ubi sunt?*—where are the glories of the past?—returns frequently in his writings). Two conflicting aspects of Petrarch's achievement as restorer of the past lay claim to our attention: his objective and detailed understanding of Roman history and of the distance which separated it from his own day, a perception which has earned for him the title of first modern historian; and his intensely subjective identification with certain figures of antiquity and the world in which they lived, an anachronistic community of spirit which yet gives to his humanism something of the sense which that term enjoys today.

In the real world of fourteenth-century politics, where Rome, deserted by the papacy, lay half in ruins and torn by the struggle for power between warring factions of the nobility, notably the Colonna and Orsini families, Petrarch's concern with its past glory is especially significant. It is not simply that he admired its civilisation and described its marvels and monuments, finding inspiration in them for his own literary endeavours, documenting outstanding individuals such as Scipio and Julius Caesar in the *De viris illustribus*, or bringing Scipio poetically to life again in the *Africa*. Rather, Roman heroes and Rome itself came to represent for him an ideal of civic virtue and world government capable of re-creation in his own day; the substance of his scholarship became a programme for action, and the core of his studies drew him directly into contemporary politics. Nowhere is this clearer than in his curious involvement with Cola di Rienzo.

Son of a Roman taverner, nine years Petrarch's junior and trained, like him, as a lawyer, Cola was like him a dedicated antiquarian with a passion for the relics of Rome's past. He was also an outstanding showman, a forceful demagogue, a visionary deeply influenced by contemporary mystical movements and a born leader with a streak of insanity. Certain parallels between his career and that of Mussolini are inescapable.

He first crossed Petrarch's path in 1343, when, as the result of a popular uprising in Rome in which he had played some part, he came to Avignon as a representative of the Roman people to seek the Pope's approval for a new form of democratic government to replace the rule of the barons in the eternal city. In May 1347 he was involved in a second uprising which culminated in his being named as one of the two Rectors of the city, and shortly afterwards was appointed Tribune by popular acclamation and granted dictatorial powers, all of which he accepted in the conviction that he was acting as an instrument of the Holy Spirit. By June of that year he was summoning all the cities of Italy to send delegates to Rome and provide for the peace and security of a united and holy Italy, calling himself Nicholas the Serene and Clement, Tribune of Liberty, Peace and Justice, Liberator of the Holy Roman Republic; in July he adopted a legal principle that the Roman people should revert to their ancient rights of sovereignty, thus annulling everything that had taken place over the preceding ten centuries; on 1 August he was knighted with a splendid display of neoclassical pomp which included ritual bathing in the font of Constantine, and on the 15th of that month he was solemnly crowned Tribunus Augustus in sextuplicate on the Capitoline. And so it went on. But by 15 November he had abdicated, and the great (and strangely proto-Fascist) revival of the Roman Republic was at an end.

These glittering and traumatic events inspired an enormous and initially uncritical enthusiasm in Petrarch. Here was a man sharing his love of antiquity, his interest in ruins, inscriptions and coins, his admiration for Livy, and his belief in the ideal of Rome, and here was a man capable of bringing that ideal to life again by liberating the city from foreigners and tyranny, and of re-creating Italy. Petrarch even offered to postpone work on the *Africa* in order to turn his pen to Cola's cause, and longed, he said, to join him in Rome to carry on the struggle (v 38). Six letters, all of them ultimately excluded from the canon of the *Familiares* (v 38, 40, 48; sn 2, 3, 4), ringing with calls for the restoration of peace, liberty and the golden age, bear witness to Petrarch's excitement and involvement in an upheaval which really only lasted six or seven months and yet seemed to epitomise his wildest antiquarian dreams: the unification of Italy through the re-creation of its ancient centre, Rome.

But the realities were different: the numerous city-states of the peninsula had never been further from uniting, and the revolution in Rome did little to re-establish its former supremacy. Petrarch burned his fingers badly: two members of the Colonna family, to whom he owed so much, were killed by Cola's forces; the Tribune's increasingly pathological behaviour became a source of severe embarrassment and agitation to the papacy, and in 1352, after some years of exile and imprisonment, he was finally excommunicated and brought to Avignon to be tried for heresy. When, that August, Petrarch wrote recalling these circumstances to his friend Francesco Nelli (f xiii 6), he betrayed a certain cooling of interest, regretting the heat of his attachment, and Cola's errors, yet maintaining that the Tribune's only real sin was to have wished to restore Rome as the seat of Empire, and to have failed. We do not know whether he intervened on his behalf, but by the following year Cola had been released and returned to favour, and on 1 July 1354 he re-entered Rome as a Senator to rule in the name of the Pope. Three months later he had been lynched by a Roman mob and Petrarch's revivalist dream was forever extinguished.

Yet the real conviction behind his involvement in this extraordinary chain of events—that Rome should be restored (anachronistically, but in keeping with medieval thinking, not merely as Republic but as the centre of a now Holy Roman Empire)—was a constant concern of his active life. From the 1330s, when he addressed two metrical letters (E I 2, 5) to Pope Benedict XII urging him to return the papacy to Rome, and wrote a number of Italian lyrics echoing the same theme, until the very end of his life, he continued to press for what was the logical political expression of his deepest-held scholarly beliefs. He sent Benedict's successor Clement VI a metrical letter on the subject in 1342 (E II 5), but it was particularly Pope Urban V (1362–70) whom he assiduously plied with prose letters, advancing endless arguments ranging from the political and spiritual advantages of Rome over Avignon to the superior quality of Italian wines, in the attempt to persuade him to restore the papacy to its historic seat (S VII 1, IX 1, XI 1,16,17; V 3). His excitement when Urban did finally travel to Rome in 1367 was only matched by his disappointment when he failed to remain there. Sadly, Petrarch died just too soon to hear of Gregory XI's definitive return in 1376, but was thus spared the knowledge that a move which he could only conceive of as propitious would result in the creation of a rival papacy at Avignon and a Schism which was to have catastrophic consequences for the Church.

His correspondence with Urban V had to some degree been foreshadowed, especially in its concern for Italy, by his repeated attempts in the 1350s, at the very time when he had clearly finally decided to leave France and return definitively to his native land, to persuade Charles IV of Bohemia to cross the Alps into Italy. Three major letters (F X 1, XII 1, XVIII 1), written at approximately yearly intervals between early 1351 and the end of 1353, and strategically placed at the opening of three different books of the *Familiares*, appeal to Charles to establish his Empire in Rome. Another, similarly placed (F XIX 1), marks his arrival in Italy with joy; yet another (F XIX 12) reproaches him bitterly with leaving only shortly after his coronation as King of Italy at Milan on 6 January 1355, at which Petrarch must have been present; in 1356 he even travelled to Prague to see him, and in 1361 wrote him yet another letter (F XXIII 2) on the theme of the restoration of the seat of Empire.

Taken together with his efforts to influence the Pope, these initiatives represent Petrarch's boldest political undertaking (though the letters themselves, as a formal, and edited, record of events, presumably represent only a part of his efforts). It is worth noting, however, the degree to which he was above all concerned with ideas—and arguably anachronistic ones—rather than with the realities of practical politics. But even Charles seems to have perceived the idealised nature of his march into Italy and his coronation, seeing them as symbolic gestures intended more to re-establish Imperial prestige than to lead to any significant intervention in Italian politics: he was quick to withdraw as soon as the going became difficult.

Yet for Petrarch the whole topic of Rome and Italy was a fertile one: his lyrics and certain of his eclogues and polemical *Invective* abound with references to the beauties of Italy, its natural and cultural superiority to France, the present distressed state of Rome and its potential as capital of the world. His triple concern, from his early forties onwards, with papacy, Cola's revolution, and Empire can be seen as the logical outcome of his scholarly reading and writing in his thirties: affairs of state arising from literary study and in their turn generating ample material for writing, whether committed and polemical or imaginative and poetic.

The same is perhaps less true of his other diplomatic activities, principally missions to Italy undertaken on behalf of Pope Clement VI in 1343 and 1347, and numerous journeys and negotiations at the behest of the Visconti under whose patronage he was living in Milan in the 1350s and early 1360s. To these commitments we owe a number of letters, generally carefully elaborated accounts of what took place, and certain speeches, notably one delivered to the French King Jean le Bon at Paris in 1361, congratulating him on his return from English captivity, and exploring the theme of Fortune in a way which obviously aroused interest in French intellectual circles. But we come closer to Petrarch's most characteristic concerns in the context of his efforts between 1351 and 1354 to bring an end to the war raging between the Venetians and the Genoans, where his letters (F XI 8, XIV 5, XVI 16, XVII 3,16, XIX 9,18) bear witness to his deep desire for peace, not simply between cities, but in Italy at large, and within himself. 'If Rome is torn apart, what is the state of Italy? And if Italy is deformed, what future life is there for me?' he asks elsewhere (F VII 5), revealing the identification of his own state with that of his country. Not surprisingly, then, what in the letters is a topical theme becomes a significant literary motif in other writings; the search for tranquillity which inspires, for instance, the *De vita solitaria* and many of the poems of the *Canzoniere* is at once a genuine desire for an end to strife and a central psychological element in the image of himself which he projects:

> Datemi pace, o duri miei pensieri!
> Non basta ben ch'Amor, Fortuna e Morte
> mi fanno guerra intorno e'n su le porte,
> senza trovarmi dentro altri guerrieri?

> Give me peace, oh cruel thoughts! Is is not enough for Love, Fortune and Death to besiege me all around, and even at my very gates, without my finding other enemies within myself? (C 274)

That Petrarch, far from withdrawing from the active life, was fully aware of the potential of the pen for polemical as well as for scholarly purposes need hardly be stressed: quite apart from the letters so far mentioned, there are numerous others written on behalf of friends or patrons for whom he was employing his literary skills. He wrote besides, still in the guise of letters, a number of small treatises on subjects of general concern, such as the education of princes (F XII 2), the qualities of a good leader (S IV 1) or the proper governance of the state (S XIV 1), and showed himself thoroughly conversant with the whole spread of European politics (F XV 7); he wrote *Invective* against doctors, or those who criticised him for serving those 'Lombard tyrants', the Visconti, or for his philosophical views (I), or those who maintained that France was superior to Italy, and he devoted a good deal of vituperative zeal to the vices of Avignon, the new Babylon. Nineteen purportedly anonymous prose letters gathered into a collection called *Sine nomine*, a sequence of three sonnets (c 136–8), two eclogues (B VI–VII) and innumerable references in his other works reveal his obsession with the moral decay at the heart of the Church, and provide at the same time one of the ethical justifications for his desire to see it return to its sources in Rome.

Yet characteristically Petrarch was to reveal, and to exploit for literary purposes, an awareness that his very concern with such issues, as indeed all *negotium*— political commitment and·the affairs of princes, popes and statesmen—was a distraction from the proper aim of Christian contemplation, and above all destructive of that *otium*—tranquillity and literary recreation—which he valued most highly. This insight constitutes an important theme in his writings (and thus, as Augustinus frequently reminds Franciscus in the third book of the *Secretum*, generates further vain effort); in all his major moral works, in many of his letters, and inevitably in the later *Trionfi* devoted to death and eternity, Petrarch constantly decries the vanity of involvement in the life of action and laments the time lost thereby to his studies. Indeed the concomitant praise of the solitary life and its virtues and benefits compared with the trials of life in society (and most particularly in Avignon) was to become one of his most fertile topics.

His principal treatise on the subject is the *De vita solitaria*. The first book systematically explores the advantages of withdrawing into the country in search of solitude: liberty, self-possession, peace of mind and body for study and spiritual advancement, together with the beauties of natural landscape and the absence of all the inconveniences of urban and social life; the second and third discuss innumerable figures of the past, ranging from Adam and Abraham to the philosophers, poets and statesmen of antiquity, who had tasted the joys of solitude and reaped its benefits. Somewhat similarly, the *De otio religioso*, addressing itself to the Carthusian monks of his brother's community at Montrieux, begins by comparing the peace of the religious life with the ceaseless, and senseless, commotion of secular society. The same themes repeatedly recur in Petrarch's prose and verse letters, the *Sine nomine*, *Bucolicum carmen* and *Invectiva contra medicum*; they are equally constantly present in the *Canzoniere*, and must have been a regular element in his conversation: he even records that he defended the solitary life in discussions with Charles IV in 1354 or 1355 (F XIX 3).

Lest it be thought, however, that his quest for solitude was self-indulgent, Petrarch is at pains on occasions to warn against idleness (VS II 14) or the ivory-tower attitudes of scholars (F XVI 16), and, when it suits his book, can discourse at great lengths upon the turbulent and unquiet state of nature (RF II pr); in the *Secretum*, Augustinus more than once admonishes Franciscus for the arrogance and failure to come to terms with his problems which have led him to seek a life apart from other men (SEC II 96, III 172). It is moreover made abundantly clear in the *De vita solitaria* that the solitary life and the tranquillity that goes with it are in fact peopled with books and friends, a privileged place for spiritual and literary activity.

Thus it is perhaps not simply because of a new appreciation for them that Petrarch lavishes so much description upon the beauties of nature. Many of the delightful evocations of his garden at Vaucluse and the surrounding countryside teem with nymphs and dryads, and other mythological companions. His 'transalpine Helicon', as he calls it, is part real garden, but part poetic exercise, for he was careful to plant it with good literary trees such as laurels and beeches which might encourage Apollo and his Muses to wander there. And it is poetry that prevails: more than a dozen Latin metrical epistles, and a significant number of the sonnets and *canzoni* in the *Canzoniere* celebrate the joys of landscape and countryside.

Yet however self-consciously literary Petrarch's treatment of them may be, the merits of withdrawal into rural isolation and the full enjoyment of an unspoiled natural environment are far from being purely literary themes. It is a fundamental feature of his career, to which he deliberately draws attention in his *Letter to Posterity*, that most of his major works were conceived of and begun while he was living at Vaucluse: the *Africa*, *De viris illustribus*, *De otio religioso*, *Secretum*, *Bucolicum carmen* and *Psalmi penitentiales* all owe their beginnings, and in some cases even their completion, to those fertile hills north of Avignon, as do a substantial number of Petrarch's prose and verse letters and of his vernacular lyrics. He consistently did seek solitude (though he was almost always surrounded by friends), whether in Provence as an escape from Avignon, or at Selvapiana in the Apennines where he spent his summers away from Parma, or in a house close to the church of Sant'Ambrogio on the extreme outskirts of Milan, or finally in his hilltop home at Arquà. And he consistently found solitude, in the company of those books which were his dearest companions, the most favourable context for study.

When in his tenth eclogue he casts himself in the role of Silvanus, an inhabitant of the woods and cultivator of laurels, or instructs himself in a marginal note in the manuscript which he had discovered of the *Oratorical Institutions* of the Roman educator Quintilian to answer that author's objections to the solitary life (and later notes there that in his *De vita solitaria* he had done his best to reply!), as when he plants laurel trees in his garden, or climbs Mont Ventoux and admires the view, or laments in the most elegant literary form that pressure of business which prevents him from writing, Petrarch is enacting, in a remarkably self-aware way, the contradictions of his own life and works and of the wholly symbiotic relationship between them. We have seen that the contemplative life, and the reading and writing which it engendered, led to his involvement in the active life of the fourteenth century; it was that involvement which, even as he blamed it for impeding his writing, led to the elaboration of a total work in which life and literature are inseparably interwoven.

4 The poetic life

Yet a further contradiction might appear to arise between those scholarly and worldly pursuits with which this book has until now been concerned, and Petrarch's activity as vernacular love-poet. The present chapter will focus upon his poetry, the Italian part of which is the best-known aspect of his creativity, in an attempt to explore the contradictions which it undoubtedly does reveal, but at the same time to dispel the myth of a radical divide between lyrics, scholarship and life. For if the solitude of Vaucluse engendered works of learning, it also provided the space and time, and the material, for a considerable body of imaginative verse, both Italian and Latin, verse which reflects all the psychological and intellectual patterns so far observed, and others besides, but which also constitutes an essential element in Petrarch's literary elaboration of his active life: the figure of the scholar as poet laureate.

The idea of coronation was one which, he later claims, came to him at an early age (RM I 37), perhaps as a result of hearing of the ceremony at which the poet Albertino Mussato was crowned with laurels at the University of Padua in 1315, or of the proposal to honour Dante similarly some four years later at Bologna. It is probable too, that his reading, and particularly of the late Latin poet Statius, who twice mentions coronation with laurels in his epic *Achilleid*, was partly responsible for an interest to which he gave expression in a number of his writings which can be ascribed with some certainty to the 1330s (F II 9, IV 2, 16; C 7, 23). Yet this interest was to become almost an obsession, and the mere idea of coronation gradually developed into a major project, comparable to Cola di Rienzo's later re-enactment of Roman ritual: to imitate, and thus to resuscitate, antiquity by being crowned with laurels on the Capitoline in Rome. It is perhaps especially significant that Petrarch should have ignored the historical sources which spoke of the coronation of poets with ivy (and even have taken issue with Servius on this point in a marginal note in his precious Virgil manuscript); whether he deliberately confused the poetic crown with the laurels traditionally reserved for Emperors, or whether he had already perceived the strategic value of the laurel, it was the laurel that he desired quite as much as the lady Laura to whom the *Canzoniere* is devoted, and the laurel, as we shall see, that was to structure much of his poetry.

It is perhaps not altogether surprising that almost no evidence remains of the efforts Petrarch must have made to bring his dream to reality. What we do have, however, is a remarkable letter to his patron Cardinal Giovanni Colonna dated 1 September 1340 (F IV 4), telling how by an extraordinary coincidence he received two invitations to be crowned laureate within hours of each other on that very day, one bidding him to Rome, and the other to Paris. We may have doubts as to the strict veracity of his account (though in the letter Petrarch says that he is enclosing the two invitations as proof), and we may question the sincerity of the hesitations he expresses in another letter written a few months later (F IV 6) as to the moral and intellectual virtues of the laurels, but we cannot ignore the significance of his decision to accept the Roman invitation, nor can we dispute his sense of organisation and timing. For on 6 April 1341, after a somewhat academic oral examination conducted by King Robert in Naples, Petrarch entered Rome, and two days later, on Easter Sunday, he was crowned poet laureate on the Capitoline and declared a citizen of Rome. It was an extraordinary achievement: an almost unprecedented re-enactment of the classical past in the centre of the classical world, and a wholly unparalleled act of self-aggrandisement.

It is the more remarkable if we consider how little Petrarch had apparently done, or at least written, to deserve such a signal accolade; as far as we can tell, scarcely more than a dozen Latin verse letters and a handful of Italian poems (at the time considered unworthy of a serious scholar) had ever left his study by 1340. So that however strikingly novel his habit of addressing his friends in hexameters may have been, he was still very much at the beginning of his career. It seems probable indeed that he was crowned less for achievement than for promise, and that the most significant element in that promise was his grandiose project, which was never to be fulfilled, for an epic poem, the *Africa*, conceived a few years earlier at Vaucluse. At the same time, it is likely that his scholarship and historical skills helped to earn him the reputation that he coveted, and it is certain that the ceremony in Rome not only endowed him with a title which has endured to this day, but also furnished him with substantial material for literary effort.

The first fruit of this is the Oration which he delivered at the ceremony itself, a discussion of the nature of poetry drawing on numerous classical authorities. In it, he expounds the difficulties of the poet's task, and the sweetness of his rewards: personal glory and the immortality of his name; he dwells too on the properties of the laurel and the allegorical function of poetry, which was to take real events and to transform them by means of 'oblique figures of some beauty' into things of a different kind (a programme which seems to have applied as much to his life as to his art). Here, as indeed in the ceremony itself, what is important is the high cultural status conferred upon the poet, for which Petrarch found ample evidence in antiquity, and which colours his thinking and writing throughout his career: some eighteen months before his death he was still to declare that poetry was the noblest of the arts (s xv 11), and almost until his dying day he continued to write poetry, whether in Latin or Italian.

Petrarch had begun to compose verse in childhood. The first piece to have survived is a Latin elegy upon his mother's death (E 1 7), written when he was fourteen or fifteen, and much later inserted into his collection of metrical epistles; the earliest of these can be dated to 1331. His first datable Italian poems belong to the decade from 1326 to 1336, which was to be his most prolific period of sustained lyric writing, and was also to see the composition of the first of the *Trionfi* and the conception of the *Africa*, which he locates in Holy Week 1333; that he continued to write and reflect upon poetry is clear from the mass of his lyrics, but also in particular from his first eclogue, a verse dialogue on poetry, probably begun at Vaucluse in 1346. Nor was this merely (as he would later have us believe) the result of youthful error; his poetic activity continued. The *Africa* seems finally to have been abandoned only early in the 1350s; the eclogues grew from one to twelve and became the *Bucolicum carmen* over some ten years, often to be retouched between 1357 and 1366; the metrical epistles began to be gathered into a composite work in the later

1340s, yet were only completed (if ever they were) some twenty years later; the *Trionfi* increased and multiplied throughout the 1340s and 1350s, and were not finally rounded off until the last year of Petrarch's life; the organisation of the Italian lyrics into a collection began in the second half of the 1330s, and that collection was to evolve continuously until his death.

Little wonder then that all Petrarch's poetry is marked by certain characteristic themes, images and concerns. Indeed to consider the *Canzoniere* in isolation from his Latin verse is to do both the poem and the poet a grave injustice, for behind all his writings lie a single culture, that of the giants on whose shoulders he was perched, and a single creative purpose: to transcend the achievement of those giants.

In the case of the *Africa* the desire to make poetry of history and in so doing to give the exemplary Scipio his own epic poem, celebrating not simply his warrior prowess but also his virtues of temperance and chastity, and his love of solitude, links Petrarch's personal attachment to this particular hero with his literary purpose of imitating (and perhaps, by combining Livy's history with Virgil's poetry, of outdoing) the classics. If he failed to complete the poem, it is perhaps because his aspirations were too great: his epic was to contain not merely battle scenes and historic confrontations, but a history and topography of ancient Rome, prophetic dreams and an allegory of Truth, a character-study of its protagonist, and finally a love-story, of Massinissa and Sophonisba, to echo that of Dido and Aeneas.

Petrarch, for all his talents as poet and historian, was not a gifted narrative writer, particularly when the story to be told was not his own; nor, for all his remarkable powers of introspection, was he a penetrating observer of the psychology of others. Thus his Scipio, albeit exemplary, is wooden, too perfect a synthesis of Roman warrior and Christian saint to be credible; his lovers are unconvincing, and their affair, despite occasional evocations of the lyric passion of the *Canzoniere*, lacking in fire; his Sophonisba's beauty a pale rhetorical shadow of the elusive charms of Laura. The verse, however measured in its Virgilian echoes, cannot carry the burden of such polymorphic purpose. The admiring description of Rome (A VIII 862–951) or the programmatic discussion of poetry attributed to Ennius (A IX 78–123) are frequently ponderous in their abstraction; it is only occasionally, in treating favourite general themes such as the passing of time and the futility of effort, or in the moving lament on the death of Hannibal's brother Mago (A VI 885–918), that Petrarch's poetry shines.

It is, however, characteristic and significant that a substantial part of the ninth book should be devoted to the discussion of poetry (in terms closely reminiscent of those used in the Coronation Oration), and of the role of the poet as transmitter of culture, for we encounter the same concerns in the *Bucolicum carmen*. These twelve eclogues, poetic dialogues in which idyllic characters discuss topical matters in allegorical terms, owe their conception, mode and style to Virgil, though their verse bears frequent traces of Petrarch's other classical reading, notably of Ovid and Claudian. But behind the veil of pastoral fiction, their subject-matter is authentically Petrarchan. While some deal with what might be termed current affairs, events close to the author's heart such as the death of King Robert (B II), the state of Rome and the rise of Cola (B V) or the corruption of the papal court (B VI–VIII), others focus on issues with which he was even more intimately concerned. The first, for instance, is a discussion between Silvius and Monicus (identifiable as Petrarch and his brother Gherardo) on the relative merits of sacred and profane poetry, in which Virgil and Homer prevail over the Psalms; the third is a poeticised account of the coronation, where the nymph Daphne leads her worshipper, the budding poet Stupeus, to Mount Olympus, home of Apollo and the Muses, and having reminded him of the illustrious precedent of Scipio, crowns him with the laurels which are her emblem; the eighth dramatises Petrarch's parting from his patron Giovanni Colonna, and his departure from Provence, in 1347. The tenth, and longest, tells of the death of the laurel caused by the plague which swept Europe in 1348: the demise at once of the beloved and of all classical poetry, leaving Silvanus—Petrarch—as sole surviving poet to carry the tradition on; the eleventh continues the lament for Laura's death, disguising her this time as the nymph Galathea.

To us, these poems often seem laboured, their allegorical garb tedious; we cannot share the enthusiasm of the fourteenth- and fifteenth-century commentators for solving the riddles which they pose. Yet for Petrarch, who constantly states that the more difficult poetry is to write, and understand, the more valuable it is, they undoubtedly represent an enterprise of high significance. The evidence of his autograph manuscript and the various letters associated with the eclogues shows that they were something of a testing-ground for his theories on literary imitation, and that the tenth in particular was intended to be both a celebration of poetry and a repository for his very considerable knowledge of classical poetry, much of it owed to Ovid. As in the *Africa*, however, the truly poetic moments are few and far between, and again represent familiar concerns: the passing of time and the fragility of human life and endeavour: a classicising lament on the death of the beloved.

The same essential elements of Petrarch's poetic autobiography, pressed in the *Bucolicum carmen* into a literary mould of unusual artifice, emerge more freely, and often with a purer lyricism, in his metrical *Epistole*, a collection finally totalling sixty-six pieces, not all of them genuine letters, divided into three books. There is no readily perceptible logic to the structure other than the most approximate of chronological sequences; they should be seen rather as constituting a kind of intimate poetical anthology whose real unity comes from the multiple facets of the writer's personality that they illuminate. A number of them are frankly, if not quite spontaneously, autobiographical: discussions of Petrarch's way of life, his shifting state of mind, his health and declining years, his love, his reading and his gardening. Some lament the deaths of patrons or friends, or make poetry of small day-to-day realities, often associated with the solitude of Vaucluse: fishing in the Sorgue, the effects of a storm on his garden, or the gift of a dog:

> Hunc michi digressus supremaque verba paranti
> solamen comitemque vie largiris . . .

> (As I was preparing to say my farewell and leave, you gave him to me as a consolation and companion for my journey . . .) (E III 5)

Others dwell on the general themes implied by his own experience: the pleasures of the simple life, the beauties of nature, the trials of travel and exile, mortality and the onward rush of time:

> Heu michi, quid patior? quo me violenta retor-
> quent
> fata retro? Video pereuntis tempora mundi
> precipiti transire fuga, morientia circum
> agmina conspicio iuvenumque senumque nec
> usquam
> tuta patet statio; non toto portus in orbe
> panditur, optate non spes patet ulla salutis.

(Alas, what must I suffer? Why does violent fate drive me back? I see the headlong flight of time as the world declines, I see the multitude of young and old dying around me; nowhere does it seem safe to stay; no safe port offers itself in all the world, no hope appears of the salvation that I desire) (E I 14)

Yet others illustrate more literary topics, but ones which we recognise as an integral part of their author's intellectual experience; book II, which opens with a poetic account of his coronation, has many letters devoted to the topic of poetry, of the reading and the writing of it, and of its high importance. Finally, certain pieces deal with the more public themes of Petrarch's active life, and notably with praise of Italy (one celebrated epistle, beginning 'Salve, cara Deo tellus, sanctissima salve/tellus tuta bona' (Hail, land beloved of God, hail, most holy, safe and good land, E III 24) is actually addressed to his native land), with lament at its present sorry state, and with exhortations to the Pope to return to Rome.

None of this will be unfamiliar to anyone who has dipped into the *Canzoniere*. The language may be different, but the themes, the interests, the images, the sources and the poetic personality behind them, are the same. It might therefore come as something of a surprise to find Petrarch explicitly rejecting his Italian lyrics in his Latin writings (F VIII 3, XXI 15), describing as juvenile ineptitudes a work to which he himself gave the title of Vernacular Fragments. Assessing these 'trifles' in 1372, he speaks of 'much that calls for forgiveness', and pleads that his age be taken into account to explain 'the varied nature of the work, the inconstant passion of love into which it plunges from the start, and the awkwardness of the style, for I wrote much of it before I reached maturity' (S XIII 10). But these are scholarly commonplaces: his frequently stated repentance for the follies, both amatory and literary, of his youth, is an integral part of the image of himself which he elaborates, and which he even formulates in the vernacular in the *Trionfi*, as we shall see in the next chapter. The scholar in him, and his erudite acquaintances, no doubt esteemed his Latin poetry more highly, and on several occasions he wrote passionately in defence of it against the strictures of hostile critics, yet he never really troubles to defend, other than in the most apologetic terms, the outstanding sequence of Italian poems which has most clearly endeared him to posterity.

The *Rerum vulgarium fragmenta*, to give the *Canzoniere* its authentic title, consist of 366 poems. The majority of these are sonnets (of which there are 317) or shorter forms: seven *ballate* and four *madrigali*; in addition there are longer pieces interspersed: nine *sestine* (stanzaic poems with a complex rhyme-scheme of six repeated words, numbering thirty-nine lines), and twenty-nine longer *canzoni*, ranging up to 169 lines in length. All this tells us little, other than that there is, in strictly metrical terms, a good deal of homogeneity, and very little innovation. The innovation—and it was a striking and immensely influential one—lay rather in the idea of uniting disparate pieces into a single coherent, and highly wrought, collection; it was only after a good number of poems had been written that Petrarch decided to collect them, and his conception of the finished whole was to evolve continuously throughout his career. It would appear that at a relatively early stage, probably in 1347, barely a decade after the formulation of the earliest collection, he determined that this poetic structure should be a bipartite one: a first, and longer section bearing on his love during Laura's lifetime; a second relating to its survival after death. By that date (that is, before the date assigned to Laura's death) he had already written the sonnet 'Voi ch'ascoltate in rime sparse il suono' which was to stand at the beginning of the collection, and the *canzone* 'I'vo pensando, e nel penser m'assale' (C 264) which was to open the second part, and had assigned them to their respective places.

It is a peculiar feature of Petrarch's creativity that it invites study as much of the process by which it became as of what it finally became; and this not merely because the literary product, however outstanding, is often not finished, or if it is, is deeply elusive and polyvalent in its meaning, but also because Petrarch has obligingly bequeathed to us the material for such study: autograph drafts and manuscripts, marginal notes, erasures and emendations. In the particular case of the *Canzoniere*, a good deal of scholarly attention has been devoted to its origins and genesis, its evolution and the continuous process by which it was enlarged, edited and recast. For present purposes, it is sufficient to know that such a process took place: that in one sense the work as a whole was never finished, but constantly in a state of flux (at the time of his death, Petrarch was still rearranging the final section of poems). It follows that it is impossible to interpret it as a single authoritative statement uttered at a particular moment. The *Canzoniere* changes with Petrarch: it is a paradigm of the development, uncertainty and sense of mortality which we have seen reflected in his Latin works. At the same time, however, it contributes decisively to making of those very features an essential part of our experience of the poet.

As Petrarch himself declared, these poems are fragments. They do not constitute a sequential narrative, though they do purport to reflect a chain of events and their consequences: the poet's first meeting with Laura in 1327, his long-suffering love for her, her death twenty-one years later to the day, and his continued devotion to her, tempered increasingly by repentance and the desire for salvation. In so far as there are facts here, he is careful to document them, both in certain of his letters where he protests their truth (E 1 6; F II 9), and in a brief note on the flyleaf of his Virgil manuscript, beginning: 'Laura, illustrious for her own virtues and long celebrated in my poems, first appeared to my eyes in my early manhood in the church of St Clare in Avignon, in the 1327th year of our Lord, on 6 April, at the early morning service. And in the same city, in the same month of April, on the same 6th day, at the same first hour in the year 1348, her light was taken from that of this world . . .'

The details look a little too carefully arranged, especially when we remember that Petrarch's entry into Rome for his coronation on 6 April 1341 is placed so precisely two-thirds of the way through this tenacious love-affair. They may well not be historically accurate, but the fiction that they represent is far more important than any chronological nicety, for it is not only a fundamental element in the underlying structure upon which Petrarch built the whole edifice of the *Canzoniere*, but also the central core of his spiritual self-construction. Of the realities of this love-affair we know nothing (even if a diligent sixteenth-century poet and scholar, Maurice Scève, identified Laura as Laure de Sade, a distant ancestress of the infamous Marquis), but of its literary elaboration we are left in no doubt. The lyric love of the *Canzoniere* is an outstanding imaginative creation.

A number of strategically placed poems give us the main dates. The sixth of April 1327 is identified (incorrectly, but significantly) with Good Friday in the third sonnet; later poems chart succeeding years, notably such key anniversaries as the seventh, fourteenth and twenty-first, the date of death (c 30, 101, 336). In all some twenty sonnets and *canzoni* contain precise chronological references which measure the passing of time from 1327 to 1358, ten years beyond Laura's demise, within the compass of the lyric structure, giving a semblance of narrative continuity even when true narrative is absent.

The opening sonnet, furthermore, itself encompasses time, representing the view of the older and wiser poet looking back over the 'juvenile errors' of the man he was, and expressing, in the most solipsistic of ways ('di me medesmo meco mi vergogno': I am ashamed of myself, within my very self) his repentance and his shame for vain hopes and vain suffering, as if the whole lyric experience the reader is about to witness is to be negated by this single reflection of a moralistic hindsight. But the theme announced so early does not become dominant until the second part of the *Canzoniere*: Love immediately appears and blunts the moral instinct; Laura is seen and at once her potential for poetry is revealed. Within the first seven sonnets her name has given rise to word play and her link with the laurels of poetry been made clear, as also her role as figure of Daphne, the nymph whom, according to Ovid's *Metamorphoses*, the sun god Apollo had loved and pursued and who had been changed into a laurel tree just in time to elude him. Yet from the start the moralist is there, for according to the habitual medieval explanation of this myth, Apollo is an allegorical figure of the man who, seeking fame and vainglory, is left only with bitter berries, and this theme too the poet anticipates.

Thus from the very beginning a major area of poetic exploration is opened out: puns on Laura and *lauro* (the laurel) become more frequent and complex elements of ornamentation, epitomised in the sonnet '*L'aura che'l verde lauro e l'aureo crine*', where the lady is fused with the breeze and the green leaves and the golden locks that it stirs. The laurel's potential as image of poetry is developed, the rivalry and parallel with the sun god as lover is pursued (c 115, 188):

> L'aura celeste che'n quel verde lauro
> spira, ov'Amor ferì nel fianco Apollo,
> et a me pose un dolce giogo al collo,
> tal che mia libertà tardi restauro . . .
>
> (The heavenly breeze that breathes in that green laurel, where Love struck Apollo in the side and placed on my neck a sweet yoke so that I am slow to recover my liberty . . .) (c 197)

Apollo merges with the sun of Laura's eyes (c 9), and in one *canzone* Daphne's metamorphosis becomes the lover's as he himself is changed first into laurels:

> Qual mi fec'io quando primier m'accorsi
> de la trasfigurata mia persona,
> e i capei vidi far di quella fronde
> di che sperato avea già lor corona,

> e i piedi in ch'io mi stetti e mossi e corsi,
> com'ogni membro a l'anima risponde,
> diventar due radici sovra l'onde
> non de Peneo ma d'un più altero fiume,
> e'n due rami mutarsi ambe le braccia!

> (What a change, when I first realised that my person was transformed and saw my hairs turning into those leaves of which I had already hoped to make my crown, and my feet, on which I stood and moved and ran, as every limb answers to the soul, becoming two roots by the waters not of Peneus but of a prouder river, and my two arms changing into branches!) (c 23)

and then into a whole sequence of classically inspired transmutations, performing as it were the ultimate imitation, not of poets but of the heroes of mythology. Finally, long after the death of Laura, and close to the end of the *Canzoniere*, she appears to him in one of many visions (c 359) and offers him the laurels of triumph, reminding him that he is still bound by '*l'aureo* nodo', the golden knot of his love.

This rich Ovidian conceit, of which only the merest outlines have been sketched here, is the most important of Petrarch's personal myths, as well as one of his most fertile sources of poetic inspiration. Within it he develops a desire that is all suffering, eternally destined to be unrequited, that sets the lover apart from other men, alienating him even from himself, and can only lead to death. It is a love deeply paradoxical in its nature, and in its effects and its expression, whether articulated as the icy fire of the poet's sensations

> Dentro pur foco et for candida neve,
> sol con questi pensier, con altre chiome
> sempre piangendo andrò per ogni riva . . .

(All fire within, but outwardly white snow, alone with these thoughts, with hair changed, I shall always go weeping along every shore) (C 30),

or in the tensions of sonnets now celebrating, now regretting his attachment, longing now for passion, now for peace. These contradictions are symptomatic of the lover's unstable state and point at the same time to the elusiveness, almost the absence, of the lover. There is no strong unifying narrative or poetic voice; rather we have multiform modulations reflecting the different facets of an imaginative experience. The poet, like his poetry, is in perpetual flux. Thus we encounter the familiar themes of the passing of time and the fragility of all things mortal, the vanity of human joys and aspirations, the onward movement of life's journey in search of a peaceful harbour, the flight from the vulgar crowd into solitude: all aspects which we recognise as typically Petrarchan (though they are of course familiar themes in classical and medieval poetry as well), yet none of them enabling us to resolve the central paradox of Petrarch himself as distinct from the poetic persona which he projects.

As the *Canzoniere* progresses, its moral implications become more explicit. At the opening of the second part, the lover still feels unable to follow the paths of righteousness which he so acutely perceives, yet the potentially heavenly qualities of Laura in life (evoked as we have seen in the first of his sonnets (C 77) thanking Simone Martini for her portrait) emerge more and more clearly as she repeatedly appears to him after her death in dreams and visions. Suffering gives way to despair, and despair to repentance, which becomes a dominant theme. He realises that his love, in so far as it was for a mortal being, was mistaken, and that her virtue, which resisted his advances, was for his good. The death-wish increases, and with it the pious hope that he may follow her to heaven. In the final two *canzoni* of the cycle, he makes an ultimate act of contrition, placing all his hope in God, and prays to the Virgin Mary, to whom he pledges his love, for mercy and good counsel, for an end to his sorrows and a beginning to salvation.

As befits what is essentially an intimate poetic anthology, however, there is a great deal more to the *Canzoniere* than merely a love story. Just as it reflects, and even creates, one major facet of Petrarch's sensibility, so it also echoes and confirms other aspects, by now familiar ones, of his intellectual composition. There are poems on the return to Rome and in praise of Italy, one of which, 'Italia mia, ben che'l parlar sia indarno', is perhaps the first patriotic hymn of Italian vernacular literature and at the same time an urgent plea for peace (c 128), matched by savage attacks on the Babylon of the *Sine nomine* (c 136–8); others treat of fame and virtue, of the deaths of friends and patrons, of Vaucluse, the countryside and the joys of solitude. And above all, and increasingly in the second part, there are constant mentions of the topic of writing which serve to remind us of the literary self-consciousness not only of the poet, but of his poems.

The dilemma of the poet is expressed in doubly paradoxical form: he is unable to write, yet forced to write; he finds writing therapeutic, and yet it is writing that creates the suffering—love—for which only writing can provide the cure. The difficulty of matching words to things, expression to emotion, even the purported impossibility of writing, are themes introduced early in the *Canzoniere* but not fully articulated until well after the death of Laura in the poetic structure. The urge to write, on the other hand, driven on by destiny and above all by love, is much more frequently encountered: love drives him to poetry; poetry creates and preserves love. Words are the only possible medium for the expression of desire; words, as he frequently exclaims, will heal the pain caused by the desire. To this degree Petrarch here, and in other places, where he speaks of the benefits of conversation (F XIII 7; S XVII 2; B IV 46–50), seems to have anticipated the notion of the 'talking cure' so dear to modern psychoanalysis. But the truly inestimable advantage of writing is that words will earn fame for their author, and may even reserve for him a place in posterity.

Given such self-consciousness, it is evident that we shall find little that might be described as spontaneous in the lyrics of the *Canzoniere* (or indeed elsewhere in Petrarch's works): they reflect literature rather than life—two of the finest sonnets on the living Laura ('L'aura gentil, che rasserena i poggi': C 194, and 'L'aura celeste che'n quel verde lauro spira': C 197) were composed in 1368, twenty years after her death, but were fitted in to the earlier part of the sequence. Many poems are virtuoso performances by a great master of verse, or studied exercises in imitation, such as a lament on the lady's illness, rigorously based on a theme from Virgil's *Georgics* (C 31). Horace is probably the source of the writing topics mentioned above, and of images of human frailty and fleeting time, and of much else besides; the influence of Ovid, not only in matters of metamorphosis and laurels, but in the imagery of Cupid shooting arrows into the eyes of the lover, is ubiquitous. There are frequent echoes of classical poets but also of moralists and historians; Cicero in particular is responsible for the recurrent and quintessentially Petrarchan theme of the sonnet 'Solo e pensoso i più deserti campi' (C 35): the vision of the lover in his misery fleeing into solitude to avoid the paths of other men; Petrarch's scholarly reading provided endless historical examples with which to illustrate the *ubi sunt* topos: the passing of great men and their achievements, and the passing of beauty. Although it is especially in the earlier poems that we find the densest use of classical references and quotations, the habit was to stay with him to the end of his days. Yet the imitation is rarely, if ever, literal or servile; indeed it may not even always have been conscious, so deeply inscribed in his memory were the writings of antiquity.

The master craftsman, moreover, was also well aware of the vernacular traditions within which he was writing; we find echoes of Dante (even if he declares (F XXI 15) that he does not wish to imitate him), of other Italian poets of that and the preceding generation such as Cino da Pistoia and Cavalcanti, and of certain Provençal troubadours. He owed the sonnet form to his Italian forebears, and the *sestina* to Arnaut Daniel, via Dante who had named him the 'best maker of the mother tongue'; from the Provençal tradition he also borrowed the *frottola* (C 105) and *escondig* (C 206), further proof of his ability to compose formal *tours de force*. And finally, we encounter constant reminiscences of Petrarch's reading of the Bible and the Church Fathers, in particular the Psalms and the Book of Job, and of course St Augustine.

What an analysis of this kind, which is in danger of degenerating into an inventory, and an incomplete one at that, cannot convey is the quality of the amalgam; the variety which all these names suggest is the basis for an alchemical process which makes writing of reading, and the finest poetry of scholarship. Petrarch's sources are not simply outside influences drawn upon on occasion, but rather an integral part of his own literary flux, the unconscious poetic magma which, as it solidifies into lyrics which are his alone, is chiselled and shaped by the conscious critical mind of the author.

Within a deliberately chosen narrow range of formal patterns, above all the sonnet, and a carefully controlled and restricted vocabulary, constantly filed and polished to ensure its evenness, its harmony and its precision, Petrarch writes poems that are at once remarkably uniform and extraordinarily varied, as recognisable and yet as elusive as is his image of himself wherever we encounter it. Each 'fragment' of the *Canzoniere* can stand on its own, yet is part of a magnificent polymorphic whole, a structure which was Petrarch's invention and perhaps his most original legacy to poetic posterity. The relationship between the parts and the whole was, furthermore, something which never ceased to occupy him.

Yet there is in one sense no clearly defined structure to the *Canzoniere*, other than the division into two by Laura's death which imposes a certain, but not an absolute, thematic pattern on the arrangement of the lyrics. The chronological framework provided by 'anniversary' poems encompassing more than thirty-one years does not so much measure time accurately as it seeks to transcend and abolish time. It is not absolutely regular; it cannot be strictly correlated with the dates of composition of individual pieces and those placed in relation to them; it is rather a fictitious cadence which evokes the transience of love and life. The strategic dating of the first encounter on Good Friday, and of subsequent anniversaries at Easter, has led scholars to detect a calendrical structure already latent in the sequence of 366, linking major poems to religious feast-days; other complex and suggestive numerological arrangements can be observed, fascinating but finally frustrating glimpses of highly wrought artistic purpose without ultimate resolution. The *Canzoniere* is as much about poetry, and the process of writing poetry, as it is about a love-affair, a spiritual crisis and the ironies of the human condition.

Petrarch may not have earned his poetic laurels in 1341 by writing Italian verse, but what he achieved over a lifetime of lyric composition in which the laurels had a major role to play was the creation of a unique and influential literary structure, deeply rooted in the multiple traditions in which he was steeped, yet reaching far beyond them, breaking with the past and transcending it. The *Canzoniere* is the first extended poem that is not narrative in the sense that Dante's *Divine Comedy* or medieval romances were; it tells no story, and yet it creates its own dynamism and its own duration out of the juxtaposition of often static lyric fragments, constantly in evolution. It encompasses the lessons of classical and vernacular poetry, of pagan and Christian aspirations, finally fusing the pursuit of a Daphne who is all vainglory with the invocation of a Virgin who is all salvation. In articulating a passion that owes as much to literature as to love, Petrarch makes poetry of the paradoxes and the tensions of the moralist for whom antiquity and solitude alone do not suffice.

5 The moral life

'My wishes fluctuate and my desires conflict, and in their conflict they tear me apart. Thus does the outer man struggle with the inner . . .' (F II 9). Writing these words to Giacomo Colonna in 1336 Petrarch reveals, at a relatively early stage in his career, that consciousness of crisis which was to mark all his major works: the watchful eye of the moralist scrutinising his own every word and action. The most striking analysis of the inner conflict, and the most remarkable expression of his self-awareness, is his *Secretum*, which we shall be considering in the next chapter; the present one will be concerned with delineating the moral tensions experienced by the outer man.

On a scholarly level we have seen the extent to which Petrarch was devoted to what we would now call his research: to reading the works of antiquity and to writing works of his own which might reflect and even transcend them. On a more imaginative literary level, we have witnessed the energy which he devoted to depicting a love which, even if it was fictitious, reflected fundamental desires and aspirations. Both the erudite and the erotic pursuits were sources of pride for him, despite all the disclaimers which he uttered; he was evidently conscious that both committed him deeply, and could earn him fame. Yet at the same time he was aware that such worldly ambitions were an impediment to spiritual growth. It is symptomatic that in the third book of the *Secretum* Augustinus should emphasise to Franciscus that his studies were as much a cause as his love of that neglect of the inner man whose well-being was essential for salvation (SEC III 150, 156, 206, 212); his repeated denunciations of human love as a barrier between man and God are echoed in the *Trionfi* and elsewhere. Franciscus is the Petrarch who has chosen the wrong path even though he was aware of the right one, a Petrarch whom we encounter frequently in his letters (F XVII 10, XVIII 16; S IV 5; SN 15) and whose dilemma is integral to the *Canzoniere* (C 264). But Franciscus is not the whole man, for without the critical consciousness of Augustinus to contend with, his reflections would lack a dimension. It is Augustinus who makes literature of Franciscus's life.

The same complex balance between individual experience and literary elaboration is illustrated in a different way by the topic of the solitary life. Far from being simply a rhetorical theme—fleeing from love, or the crowd, or the pressures of life at court, in order to seek the tranquillity of the countryside—a theme as essential to the *Canzoniere* as to the *De vita solitaria*, *De otio religioso*, and to innumerable letters—it is equally a real reflex, a recipe for the conduct of life which, in Petrarch's withdrawal to Vaucluse, proved fertile in terms both of his literary output and of his intensive meditation upon it. Something similar may be said of the travels with which this book began: between literary topic and verifiable experience there is no clear dividing line. The realities of Petrarch's day-to-day actions, or such as we are informed of, are a mirror image of his reflection upon them; what he does is principally significant because he chooses to tell us that he does it, because of the lessons he draws from it, and because of the synthesis of lesson and life which his writings bequeath to us.

The imitation of antiquity in particular constitutes an interesting challenge for the medieval scholar. Its institutions and its literature, and the ethical values portrayed by both, were not necessarily in accord with Christianity, and indeed the fables of pagan literature had been singled out for particular condemnation by St Jerome. The multiple gods of ancient Rome could scarcely be accommodated with medieval monotheism, but nor could the stoic notion of *virtus*, which placed such stress upon the achievement of the individual, readily be assimilated to the self-denying virtues of the Catholic Church. To quote but one example with which Petrarch was to be concerned (RF II 118): Cato's suicide, much praised by Seneca as an instance of individual fortitude, could have little justification in terms of a Christian code of morals, however admirable an example it might appear. To reconcile humanism—a passion for and specialised knowledge of the classical past—with the ethical exigences of a Christian world was a cultural and intellectual problem of some magnitude, which Petrarch was one of the first to attempt to resolve without having recourse to the usual medieval escape-route of allegorical explanation.

The signs of his struggle are especially evident in his more overtly classicising Latin works. We have seen, for instance, how he sought to combine classical scholarship with Christian moral purpose in the *Rerum memorandarum libri* by grouping the exemplary words and deeds of the heroes of antiquity under the headings of the four cardinal virtues of Christianity: Prudence, Justice, Fortitude and Temperance. The same desire for reconciliation can be detected in the *Africa*. It is not simply that Scipio is intended to exemplify both Roman and Christian virtues, but also that the whole poem reflects a constant syncretistic urge to combine two largely incompatible religious and ethical systems. At its most peculiar, this is revealed in a passage where Jupiter, foreseeing the future, predicts his own reincarnation as Christ, born of a Virgin (A VII 710–24). That Petrarch was well aware of the latent tension in his epic is made clear in a letter of 1363 (s II 1) where he attempts to answer criticism of the poem by arguing that Mago's sentiments on his deathbed (A VI 889–913), moral reflection upon mortal frailty, and repentance (as much Petrarch's own as those of his fictitious re-creation of Hannibal's brother), were just as possible for a pagan as for a Christian.

One side of Petrarch, which found classical culture more engaging than that of the age in which he was born, was as we have seen articulated in his first eclogue, where Silvius declares the poetry of Homer and Virgil superior to that of the Psalms. That predilection is, however, frequently overruled by the sterner moralist represented by Augustinus in the *Secretum*, though never without a struggle. It is symptomatic of Petrarch's disingenuousness that Franciscus is not completely defeated at the end of the debate, and that his opponent is obliged to recognise his own debt to the classics, and notably to Cicero (SEC I 66). Furthermore, the case for Cicero as a proto-Christian, frequently implied in the *Secretum*, is made quite explicit in the *De ignorantia* at the end of Petrarch's life:

Cicero, read with the heart of a believer and in a balanced way, is certainly not harmful to Augustine or anyone else; on the contrary, he was beneficial to them all in terms of eloquence and to many of them in their daily lives . . . When I have to think or speak of religion, that is of the supreme truth, true happiness and eternal salvation . . . it seems certain to me that Cicero himself would have been a Christian if he had been able to see Christ or had known of his doctrine. (I 1122–4)

Similarly, although it is clearly Christianity that prevails in the *De vita solitaria*, the solitude that is urged is, in the end, especially given all the examples of antiquity in the third book, closer to a classical literary ideal than to a monastic or ascetic withdrawal from secular life, and Petrarch notes in passing that even St Jerome borrowed from a Roman author (vs II 5).

The moralist who thus haunts Petrarch's scholarship is never far removed from his love-lyrics either. At an early stage in the *Canzoniere* (c 16), the lover seeing his lady's image is compared with a pilgrim journeying to Rome to see the features of Christ imprinted on the cloth with which St Veronica wiped his face; such awareness of the confusion of earthly and heavenly desires is characteristic, and can verge on the heterodox. Although Laura is never explicitly assimilated with the Virgin Mary, the final *canzone* 'Vergine bella che di sol vestita' (c 366) confirms an implicit identification, and the heavenly features of the earthly lady are a recurrent feature of the poetry, self-consciously commented upon by Franciscus in the *Secretum* (SEC III 136). But it was not in fact within the fragmentary framework of the *Canzoniere* that Petrarch finally sought to resolve this tension, for the lover is as important in his lyrics as the moralist. The definitive elaboration of a synthesis which would fuse love, scholarship, and an orthodox moral viewpoint, was reserved for his other major vernacular work, the *Trionfi*, which was to occupy him until the very last year of his life.

In classical times, a Triumph was the celebration with which a victorious general might be honoured on his return to Rome: a procession through the city to the Capitoline in which the victor in his chariot would be preceded by his captives and spoils. Petrarch's original poetic adaptation of this ceremony, the first chapter of the Triumph of Love, was composed, in the form of a dream, at Vaucluse in the late 1330s, and showed the triumphant Cupid following a long procession of classical lovers. In the subsequent two chapters, the procession was lengthened to contain others (including the Massinissa and Sophonisba of the *Africa*, and medieval figures such as Tristan and Isolde); even Laura appears in it, and the poet too is then taken captive; in the fourth and final chapter, love-poets ranging from Virgil and Ovid to certain troubadours, Dante, Cino da Pistoia and Petrarch's friends Socrates and Lelius, are numbered among the defeated, and the Triumph ends with an evocation of the pangs and delusions of love.

For the reader, the nature of the enterprise thus far is clear, though we should remember that the various chapters were not necessarily composed in the order in which they now stand. Once again, Petrarch was attempting to make poetry of erudition, but this time within a classicising framework destined to integrate his personal—or poetic—experience into both a literary-historical paradigm and a moralistic structure. The gradual evolution of the work from one to six Triumphs, three of which are subdivided into several chapters, need not concern us here so much as the final pattern which was to emerge. After the Triumph of Love came that of Chastity: a celebration of Laura's virtue which overcomes the God of Love; now it is she who leads the procession with Cupid as sole captive. Significantly enough, Scipio, renowned for his purity, joins the virtuous ladies already part of it, and when they arrive in Rome, Laura places the laurel wreath of victory on the altar of the temple of Chastity.

The third Triumph is that of Death, and in particular over Laura on that sixth day of April, which, as we are reminded, was the precise anniversary of Petrarch's falling in love with her. Here, a long evocation of the vanity and transience of mortal things is followed by a vision in which Laura claims that she is now the one who is truly alive, whereas her lover, whose long survival on earth she predicts, is dead because of his attachment to the temporal world:

'Viva son io e tu se' morto ancora'
diss'ella, 'e sarai sempre infin che giunga
per levarti di terra l'ultima ora'

('I am alive, and you are still dead', she said, 'and will be until the hour finally comes for you to leave the earth') (TM 22–4)

Then Fame triumphs over Death, bringing with her many celebrated figures of the classical and biblical past, long since gone yet still remembered. And then Time, envious of men's fame, triumphs over Fame, inspiring another meditation upon the impermanent nature of this life. Finally, in the last Triumph, written less than a year before Petrarch died, we are vouchsafed a vision of that Eternity which will transcend all time, past and future, in an eternal present abolishing memory and hope, and promising eternal bliss for Laura's soul, and for her lover's. The final triumph to come will be in heaven.

Petrarch's achievement in the *Trionfi* is not strictly a poetic one: his handling of the *terza rima* (the metre used by Dante in the *Divine Comedy*) is not especially remarkable, except in certain passages devoted to general lyric themes such as we encounter elsewhere in his writings; erudition tends to outweigh lyrical and narrative concerns. On the other hand, this sequence of poems does represent a significant moral synthesis, a structure within which earthly love (whether real or fictitious) is given an ultimate meaning, so that Laura's role, as it evolves from the Triumph of Love to that of Eternity, can finally be seen as being to guide the poet towards that better path which he purports, in the *Canzoniere* and *Secretum* at least, to have been so reluctant to follow.

Elsewhere in his writings, however, such profane themes as love are either entirely absent or strictly subordinate to Petrarch's moral doctrine, to such a degree indeed that it is tempting to see a total contradiction between them and his Italian verse, as if the sterner tones of the Latin treatises confirmed the moralist's self-critical rejection of frivolous lyrics in the mother-tongue. The *De vita solitaria* for instance, as we have seen, has nothing to offer a lover but the joys and benefits of solitude, not the least of which is to allow time and tranquillity. On the other hand, the second and third books, with their rich anthology of famous cultivators of the solitary life, amply demonstrate Petrarch's ability to deploy the full range of his learning in pursuit of what was evidently for him an intensely personal moral theme.

The *De otio religioso*, which he began in 1347, a year after the *De vita solitaria*, develops similar arguments within a more rigorously monastic context, since his pretext for writing it was to celebrate his experience of a visit to his brother Gherardo in the Charterhouse of Montrieux. Starting from a text taken from the Psalms,

'Be still and see that I am God' (Ps. 45:11), he uses biblical and patristic quotations and examples, but also inevitably classical ones, to show that the stillness, the *otium* of religious life, is preferable to all the cares of the secular world. He surveys natural disasters and the fall of civilisations, and above all the miserable condition of man and the ill-effects of sin; he dwells on the struggle between the spirit and the flesh and the inevitability of death, and concludes, after reviewing other sects and philosophies, that the eternal life, to which the Scriptures are the surest guide, is the highest good. Were it not for the wealth of classical material and his obvious familiarity with the world of antiquity, one would hardly suspect the humanist here.

Any more than one would (but why should one?) in his seven *Psalmi penitentiales* (Penitential Psalms), contemporary with the first form of the *Secretum*, a brief and moving exploration in the style of the biblical Psalms of the themes of guilt and repentance, of days spent in deliberations and bitterness and a life wasted in the pursuit of mistaken goals. But in its self-questioning, and in the lyrical evocation in the fourth psalm of the bounties of God's creation, Petrarch's introspective and poetic gifts, and his humanity, are clear.

So far we have viewed him as a man of parts: scholar, poet and moralist, sometimes more one than the other, on occasion all three in synthesis. Despite innumerable points of similarity, echoes of theme and tone, and explicit cross-reference, however, we have in the works so far mentioned encountered no element of systematic thinking. Indeed when one considers the way in which almost all these works (with the salient exception of the *Psalmi penitentiales*, apparently penned in a single day) evolved over an extended period of time, in what often seems a random, though far from unconsidered fashion, it is not altogether surprising that system is lacking. It is rather almost as if Petrarch deliberately wished to prevent his reader from pinning down a single moment or stable point of view within the constantly evolving reflection of his own fluctuating state.

The *De remediis utriusque fortune* is unusual among his major works in that it was begun relatively late in his career, probably in his fiftieth year, and although it took twelve years to complete, does not show quite the same signs of gradual composition, evolution and piecemeal revision as his other writings. It is furthermore outstanding not merely as the most encyclopedic of his works, the major achievement of his maturity, but also as the nearest he came to a systematic statement of moral philosophy. It takes the form of 253 dialogues divided into two books, the first providing remedies for good fortune, showing that material blessings are illusory and the only real values ethical and spiritual ones, and the second providing consolation for the ills brought about by adverse fortune. The dialogue, which rarely comes to life and is little more than a rhetorical mechanism for contrasting attitudes, is carried on between Reason and Joy or Hope in the first book, Sorrow or Fear in the second; the topics covered mirror the diversity of human experience, ranging from the metaphysical to the mundane, from happiness, hope and virtue in the first book to inheritance, horses and games of chance; from grief, ingratitude, exile and death in the second to fleas, unfaithful wives, stomach-ache and gout.

JOY. What if my head is crowned with the laurels of poetry?

REASON. Seeking the truth is a high endeavour, but

seeking and decorating are two different things . . .

JOY. I have plucked the laurels for myself.

REASON. The greenest tree will wither once it is plucked unless it is immediately tended with fertile intelligence and vigilant study . . . (RF I 46)

JOY. I am enjoying a passionate love.

REASON. You will be overpowered by the snares of passion.

JOY. I am burning with a passionate love.

REASON. You are right to say burning. For love is a hidden fire, a pleasing wound, a sweet bitterness, a delightful disease, an agreeable torture, a charming death . . . (RF I 69)

SORROW. I have lost my friend.

REASON. If, as you should, you loved your friend for his virtue, then surely that is not lost, nor can it die. True friendships are immortal, for friends are never parted by any quarrel nor even by death itself; thus virtue conquers every discord and vice, and can itself be overcome by nothing.

SORROW. I have lost my friend.

REASON. When you lose other things, you have them no longer, yet when you seem to have lost friends, and anyone who is dear, then do you have them to the greatest degree . . . (RF II 52)

FEAR. What will men say of me after my death?

REASON. This is an untimely concern: you should have entertained it from your youth, for a man's reputation corresponds to what his life has been.

FEAR. What will they say about me?

REASON. What reply can I give other than that given by
Cicero, the wisest and most eloquent of men? What
others will say of you will concern them, but they
will say it all the same ... (RF II 130).

For every joy which life seems to offer, Reason has a
caution; for every misfortune, a consolation.

The second book of the *De remediis* belongs fairly
firmly to a long tradition of literature epitomised for the
Middle Ages by the *Consolation of Philosophy* of the
late Roman Christian writer Boethius. Petrarch's view,
however, appears to have been that good fortune was
more dangerous than the adverse kind (a view shared by
St Augustine and other Church Fathers, but ultimately
derived from Seneca), and in adding the first book, whose
essential theme is contempt for the material world
(another good medieval moral theme), he was in fact
giving a new dimension to the discussion of the whole
problem of Fortune. Medieval thinkers had found it
difficult to reconcile the originally classical notion of an
arbitrary fate, most usually represented by the goddess
Fortuna, blindfold and turning a wheel on which men's
lives depend, and the usual Christian belief in Divine
Providence: the guiding hand of an all-seeing and
almighty God. It was undoubtedly in this context that
Petrarch's *magnum opus* was read, and doubtless because of this that it was to become one of the most
popular works of moral philosophy of the fourteenth and
fifteenth centuries.

As we might expect, classical inspiration has a major
role to play. The protagonists of the dialogues, effectively Right Reason and the four affections or passions of
the soul, are borrowed from Cicero's *Tusculan Disputations*, and reflect a certain Stoicism in the ethical
framework which they provide for Petrarch's deliber-

ations. Furthermore, however everyday some of the topics for discussion are, they are always illustrated by recourse to the writings and historical examples of antiquity, to such an extent that the *De remediis* seems almost a compendium of all Petrarch's vast erudition. More than that, however, it is a complex statement of his moral-philosophical outlook.

On the particular subject of Fortune, Petrarch is ambivalent. He stresses that life is a perpetual struggle, and that our temporal existence constantly brings us into conflict with circumstances beyond our control and incompatible with our personalities, but he does not consistently attribute such ills to Fortune any more than to the will of God. He portrays Nature as a guiding force (and certainly believed in a determinist universe), yet sees God's overriding design as being that which shapes men's destinies; to Fortune, whose existence he denies other than as a useful name, he none the less appears to ascribe the accidental details of life; to man he allows some measure of free will, enabling him notably to sin, but also to rise above his condition by the cultivation and exercise of virtue.

Petrarch does not appear to have been adept at abstract thought. Thus, rather than being a truly systematic attempt to resolve a major philosophical problem by reconciling Christian and classical ethics, the *De remediis* is much more an anthology of practical morality, united by a concern with man's reactions to the human condition, and providing remedies for specific difficulties, armour against the individual slings and arrows by which he is assailed. The unifying theme is recognisably stoic: that the wise man will place no trust in anything but his own rightmindedness, that he will accept misfortune, and by accepting it lessen its impact, and that he will distinguish good from evil. Interestingly, moreover, the virtue constantly proposed by Reason in the dialogues does not readily conform to the categories of the Christian cardinal virtues, even if the coupled notions of temperance and fortitude so beloved of St Augustine are frequently encountered. This *virtus* is rather a classical notion: a quality of mind and body to be cultivated by study and effort, an individual ethic which will bring to the individual nobility and glory, a distinction exemplified by the lives and achievements of the great men of the past, and one which sets the good man above the common crowd. If, as we have seen, Petrarch identified with classical figures such as Scipio, it was undoubtedly with such élitist intentions and such aspirations to self-improvement.

What the *De remediis* does is to explore in minute (and often tedious) detail the practical consequences of a moral-philosophical outlook which informs many of Petrarch's other writings. Stoic attitudes, often derived from Cicero via St Augustine, are also frequently to be found in the *Secretum*, and in many of his letters; the twists of Fortune's wheel are repeatedly evoked as a graphic image of the instability of life in contexts as different as the *Africa*, love-sonnets, letters to friends, the account of the journey to Jerusalem, and the ambassadorial speech to the King of France.

At the same time, however, the long succession of dialogues opens up yet again some of the major contradictions in Petrarch's attitudes and is itself shot through with contradictions. On the one hand, following St Jerome, he declares that fate and fortune do not exist, yet on the other he constantly uses them as terms interchangeable with providence, useful tools for the instruction of ordinary men. And Reason even argues against herself from one book to the other, for she represents a mode of thought to be applied according to circumstances rather than a fixed set of truths. The truths, Petrarch says elsewhere (F XII 3), are not in books and words, but in the mind.

Thus the *De remediis* is best taken in small doses, to tell you what to do, or what to think, if you are tempted to rejoice in your possessions, your friends, your wife or your reputation, or inclined to place hope in your children or your future; equally, it will teach you to calm your grief or anxiety at such contrary events as theft or disease, or your fears of poverty, betrayal, disgrace, pain and death. It is a manual for the moral life, reflecting interestingly upon topics which we have seen to be constantly in Petrarch's mind. In it, for instance, we find Reason denouncing the collecting and study of books (RF I 43–4), while the dialogues on love and women (beautiful, noble and fertile wives in the first book, RF I 65–7; departed, importunate, immodest and sterile ones in the second, II 17–22) provide a ferociously anti-feminist counterpoint to the figure of Laura, and to that degree echo a typically medieval oscillation between the figures of the archtemptress Eve and the redeeming Virgin Mary. In the *De vita solitaria*, indeed, Eve is explicitly denounced for having ruined Adam's solitude; yet the very next section of the text provides examples of virtuous women who cultivated the solitary life (vs II 4–5). And one of the last letters in the *Seniles* (s XVII 4) is in fact a translation into Latin of the tenth novella of the tenth day of Boccaccio's *Decameron*: the story of Griselda (who was to become the long-suffering heroine of Chaucer's *Clerk's Tale*), a supreme example of feminine virtue. The exemplary discourse can be turned in either direction, for here, as in the *De remediis*, Petrarch is moralist, not poet.

But some of the moralist's finest themes, in the *De remediis* and elsewhere, are also the poet's. A fundamental message to emerge from all his writings is that of the swiftness of time, the unstable state of mortal existence, the fragility of man and all his works. In the *De remediis* it is repeatedly recalled, whether in the very first dialogue of the first book, where Reason speaks of the passing of youth, and the brevity and uncertainty of life, in the long dialogue on sorrow and unhappiness (RF II 93), where the infinite misery of the human condition is explored, or in an extended and almost lyrical (and classically inspired) evocation of the flux of the whole universe in the preface to book II:

> Of all the pleasing things I ever read or heard, almost nothing impressed itself more deeply, or clung more closely, or returned more frequently to my memory than Heraclitus's dictum: all things are ruled by strife. For thus it is, and almost everything in the world bears witness that it is so. The stars resist the swift motion of the skies, contrary elements conflict with one another: the earth trembles, the waters ebb and flow, the air is agitated and fires crackle; the winds wage eternal war, the seasons contend each with the other, and all with us ... (RF II pr).

These topics, which we find in the *De otio religioso* or the *De vita solitaria*, especially in the form of the *ubi sunt* motif—the lamentation of the passing of the glories of the past (OR II 700; VS II 14)—play a central role in Augustinus's argument with Franciscus in the *Secretum*. In the third book in particular the saint urges the sinner to examine his face in the mirror, and, considering the evidence there visible of his own decay, to meditate upon it in the context of the cosmos and the perpetual whirling of the stars (SEC III 180). Dozens of letters, particularly in the latter books of the *Familiares* and the later collection of *Seniles*, pursue similar themes. The opening letter of the final book of the *Familiares* is virtually an anthology of classical quotations on the passage of time, related here to the thirty-year span of the correspondence, the literary life as progression towards death: 'we are continuously dying, I as I write this, you as you read it, others as they listen or do not listen . . . we are both dying; everyone is dying. . .' (F XXIV I). As Petrarch grows older, his letters increasingly reflect his own passage through time, the changes in himself and the world around him, and the gradual decline of all things.

The lyric elaboration of this topic was touched on in the last chapter. The *Canzoniere* not only creates the sense of the onward rush of time by its framework of dates and anniversaries and by the retrospective vision of the poet surveying his own 'lost days', but also explores quintessential aspects of it: unrequited desire, endless and futile journeying, the approach of old age and death, unfulfilled hope for the future and even (once again a classical theme) the fragility of words:

> Per voi conven ch'io arda e'n voi respiro,
> ch'i' pur fui vostro; e se di voi son privo
> via men d'ogni sventura altra mi dole:
> di speranza m'empieste e di desire
> quand'io parti' dal sommo piacer vivo,
> ma 'l vento ne portava le parole

> (For you I must burn, and in you breathe, for I was yours alone; and if I am deprived of you no other misfortune pains me so greatly; you filled me with hope and desire when I departed, leaving that highest pleasure still alive, but the wind carried away the words.) (C 267)

Laura and her lover are prisoners of time: in the *Trionfi* its ravages and those of death will prove the vanity of mortal things in the perspective of eternity.

A similar kind of pattern can be discerned if we examine another major Petrarchan concern, fame. A number of dialogues in the first book of the *De remediis* deal with various aspects of ambition, the desire for recognition and praise arising from worldly pursuits such as writing, studying, erecting fine buildings and keeping noble company; Reason systematically argues that glory is not what it seems, and that virtue is more important (RF I 11, 44, 46–7, 92, 94, 97–9). The converse of this attitude is encountered in the second book, where disgrace, infamy and even importunate and undesired reputation are shown to be no more than empty opinion, and, what is more, the opinion of the common people, notoriously fluctuating and unreliable (RF II 24–5, 34–5, 88). Exactly the same linking of fame and popular opinion is found at the beginning of the *De otio religioso* (OR I 574), and represents a typically Petrarchan crux: the desire to outshine his contemporaries confronted by the realisation that this is the kind of vainglory betokened by the bitter berries of the laurel, and that it rests upon the most volatile and contemptible of judgements, that of the common man.

It is entirely in accordance with this conflict that ambition to win fame should loom large in Augustinus's strictures. In the third book of the *Secretum* he calls *gloria* one of the two chains which bind Franciscus to his mortal state, describing such fame as he coveted as no more than a breath of wind, and urging him to cultivate virtue instead, letting true glory follow if it will (SEC III 130–2). In the *Familiares* Petrarch frequently explores the relation between fame and the envy which it incurs (F IX *passim*, XII 3), returning to the theme again many years later in the *De ignorantia*, retorting with accusations of envy to those who accused him of ignorance (I 1034, 1128). But by that stage in his career, he was a wiser man and had absorbed the moral lesson of his own earlier writings, for he argues that fame is not worth having if it deprives one of one's tranquillity: that it is better to be called illiterate but to be good. The distance between this attitude and that of the younger Petrarch of the Coronation Oration, who not only aspired to glory but even claimed it as a just reward for poetic activity, is considerable, yet both views are indubitably his.

Tensions such as this are evident in the *Canzoniere*. The very first sonnet speaks of shame at being a subject of popular discussion, yet the whole lyric edifice, like the *Africa*, is in one sense an attempt to win acclaim. The *canzone* 'Una donna più bella assai che'l sole' reveals the poet's consciousness of his own dilemma, confessing that his devotion is to a lady who is Glory and raises him above other men, crowning him with laurels after she has foretold that he will also fall in love with Virtue (C 119). The implications for the figure of Laura are clear. Yet even at the very end of the cycle nothing is resolved, for in one of the last *canzoni*, where the poet defends himself against Love in the court of Reason, Love proclaims that it was he who made the lover famous (C 360). Only in the *Trionfi* is the conflict finally brought to an end as Time, envious of men's fame, overwhelms it, proclaiming it nothing but a second death, a further proof of mortal frailty (TT 24, 143).

In the interplay between his often self-interested attachment to the dignity of man and his profound awareness of the misery of the human condition, we might sense something of the puritan in Petrarch. Yet despite the vigilant eye of Augustinus, Franciscus remains a figure of fame. The process implied by his constant moral reflection upon the events of a lifetime, and by his constant projection of moral reflection into events whether true or fictitious, is a dynamic transformation of the fruits of scholarship and the fruits of experience into the highly structured components of an ideal vision. When Petrarch consciously reorders the ruins of Rome which he had studied and visited, in order to make high poetry of them in the *Africa*, or to evoke the glories of the past and the history of the capital of the Christian world in a letter to a friend, he is imposing a literary or ideological structure upon the realities which he had observed, and for which his curiosity was unabated. When, on the other hand, he relates his ascent of Mont Ventoux in terms which make of an exploit which may owe as much to imagination as to observation a central image of his desires and aspirations, and of his acute consciousness of his own moral and psychological weaknesses, he is creating a new ethical order out of the fragments of his experience.

The aim of the moralist was to raise his subjective experience to the level of a universal and objective truth, a task for which poetry was peculiarly well suited. But Petrarch's sense of his moral autonomy, and the need to forge an identity for himself, enabled him to go further: not merely to make a work of art out of the events of his life, but also to transform that life itself into a work of art. The following chapter will focus upon this creative propensity, a final demonstration of the bond between life and literature which makes of Petrarch one of the creators of the modern self.

6 The life as work of art

Petrarch was well aware of the potential of his own story for fiction. He several times referred to his life as *fabula*, a fable (F XIX 3; S XII 1; VS I 310), subject in the telling to the same processes of composition and structuring as any of his writings, capable of being brought to a good conclusion. He was equally aware of the literary problems which this entailed: editing and where necessary emending one's own past in order to overcome the radical divide between life and words of which Cicero had spoken (F XIV 1). And he was conscious, too, of the implications of his imitation of antiquity: of the way in which the inspiration of literature can lead to the assuming of roles, the identification with classical heroes to the adoption of a persona and a way of life possibly at variance with the present. But his persistent moral view, most clearly expressed in the *De ignorantia* when he was in his sixties, was that literature properly applied can make a man good (I 1044); and by that late stage in his career his explicit conviction was that he was born to be good rather than simply to indulge in literature.

We must now focus more closely on the characteristically Petrarchan theme which has lain behind much of what has gone before: that of making oneself into what one wishes to become, of creating an image of oneself consonant with one's aspirations. This is no ordinary ambition; it is through literature, reflecting the writer's inner life more faithfully than the random course of everyday events, that the process is realised.

Paradoxically enough, however, everyday events once they are recorded lose their random quality, and it is often in letters purporting to relate the minor details of daily life that we are able most clearly to perceive the vital fictions in the making.

Indeed, Petrarch's letters are among the most important witnesses to (and products of) his elaboration of his self. The task of building them into carefully structured collections implied eliminating many and editing or rewriting those that were selected; it also implied (despite his disclaimers, F XXIV 13) the deliberate composition of others for the sake of the structure. It is perhaps worth noting, as a sign of the self-consciousness of these texts, how many of the *Familiares* and *Seniles* are about correspondence and writing, two real and continuous activities which thus become self-generating, and how many recount, for no evident purpose other than the recounting, apparently insignificant events, or remind correspondents of experiences they had shared with Petrarch in the past: pretexts for literary and even autobiographical embellishment. From these and others we gain some idea of his awareness of what he was doing: honouring correspondents by including letters to them in his collected works, creating correspondence as a consciously literary form of real relationship, strategically re-creating the past through correspondence to make sense of it for the present, and doubtless for the future.

But the creative process has a further dimension, for letters once written, as other works of literature, may have a significant influence upon the form which life assumes. Petrarch often refers to his writings as companions to his friends, signs of his presence when he is absent, mirrors in which they may see themselves reflected and which will thus affect their readers when the writer is not present to do so himself. But letters are also mirrors for the writer's soul, acting in place of conversation as a form of therapy, allowing him to explore and unburden himself of his cares, and console himself in the absence of friends, enabling him to express desires and aspirations excluded from his less apparently autobiographical works. Thus between life and letters there is a constant interchange: life generates letters; letters generate life, or the image of a life.

Nowhere perhaps are this intricate relationship, and the wilful patterning of the structuring consciousness which does much to reinforce it, so clear as in Petrarch's account of his ascent of Mont Ventoux. The letter in which it is contained (F IV 1) is dated 26 April 1336, and purports to have been written that very evening, as he returned hotfoot or more likely footsore from the slopes, to tell how he and his brother climbed the mountain and admired the view. What it at first sight describes is Petrarch's stumbling struggle uphill by paths which appeared more attractive because they were less steep, but which often led him downhill and therefore increased his fatigue, as opposed to Gherardo's much more direct and rapid ascent. What this means, however, is that the Carthusian monk had chosen the harder path, but that it had led him to spiritual heights sooner than his brother, who was still distracted by the charms of the secular world, and had sought an easy solution. The allegory is transparent, and Petrarch makes it all the more evident as he describes how, on his arrival at the summit, the wind blew open his copy of his favourite book—St Augustine's *Confessions*, which he happened by chance to have with him—at a passage which reads: 'men go to admire the heights of mountains and the mighty flood of seas and the broad swell of rivers and the compass of ocean and the wheeling of the stars, yet to themselves they pay no heed' (*Conf.* x viii 15). This invitation to introspection is an integral part of the experience which Petrarch allows us to have of him. But it is hardly fortuitous.

To begin with, the letter is addressed to Dionigi da Borgo San Sepolcro, an Augustinian friar and theologian of some note, who had given Petrarch his copy of the *Confessions* three years before the date ascribed to the climb. The date itself, furthermore, is not without significance, being, as Petrarch reminds us, the tenth anniversary of his leaving Bologna and thus finally abandoning his legal studies. He was moreover in his thirty-second year in 1336, and Augustine's own conversion to the way of the spirit dated from his thirty-second year; Petrarch, who knew this, is careful to point out that Augustine too had happened upon a significant text which had revealed to him the folly of his former ways. That such potent parallels and weighty moral precepts were unlikely to spring to mind after a hard day's mountaineering is evident, all the more so if we bear in mind that Gherardo did not enter the Charterhouse until April 1343, seven years after the event. Only then does the comparison between the two brothers assume any function or impact, and indeed it is now generally believed that it was not until 1353 that the letter was put into its final form. Seventeen years later, a day's excursion had become a programme for life.

Even if, in the end, Petrarch never did climb Mont Ventoux, the account he wrote of his ascent is of considerable ethical and literary interest. It articulates a moral theme which we find in many other of his Latin and Italian writings—the difficulty of adopting the steeper path to the good—thereby giving tangible bio-graphical form to a spiritual crisis which evidently lasted a number of years; at the same time, it reveals the high degree of literary self-consciousness with which Petrarch portrays the essential influence of Augustine not simply on his writings, but on his life as he intended us to perceive it. If this letter is a fiction, it is a fiction quite as significant as any experience which may lie behind it.

The most explicit reflection of St Augustine's presence in Petrarch's life is, however, the *Secretum*, drafted in 1347 and reworked some six years later, the 'secret conflict of my cares' which he appears not overtly to have wished to publish during his lifetime. The conflict is embodied in a dialogue, divided into three days and carried on in the presence of Truth, between Franciscus, representing Petrarch as hero of his own story, and Augustinus, who stands not so much for St Augustine himself as for Petrarch as self-critic, the moralist trying to persuade his love-sick and ambitious *alter ego* of the folly of his ways. Read as an essay in self-analysis, their debate offers insights of a remarkably modern kind, not least because as the analysis unfolds, it can be seen to be creating the conditions for its own continuation: the *Secretum*, as it composes a self, composes itself. Pet-rarch's long meditations upon St Augustine's *Confessions* take shape in what becomes his own Confession, consciously written down to give permanence and reality to the flux and fictions which it represents. Wherever we look, the knowing and frequently dis-ingenuous or self-indulgent eye of the author glints. Augustinus sets the tone by praising Franciscus for his self-awareness at the beginning, and, when Franciscus recalls the fig tree under which St Augustine saw the light, congratulates him upon his parallel devotion to the laurel tree; as their debate draws to a close, Franciscus admits that his confessor has taken all the evidence of his misdemeanours from what he revealingly calls 'the book of my experience' (SEC III 160).

We have already encountered the moral crisis which seems to have provoked this apparently scrupulous, if self-conscious, act of contrition: Petrarch's awareness of the tension between faith and experience, between the love of God and the love of a woman, between the Christian moralist's view of the vanity of all earthly pursuits and the humanist's efforts to make of his every achievement a monument worthy of the classical past, between the knowledge that the upward path is difficult, and the desire to stand on the summit of the mountain. This awareness is born of an introspective habit expressed in Petrarch's writings as in his journeys, reflecting his deep sense of dissatisfaction with what and where he is, of aimlessness and inadequacy, feelings which continue today to be associated with intellectual activity.

Analogies between the debate in the *Secretum* and the religious practice of confession or its modern avatar, psychoanalysis, are not far-fetched, so long as we remember that both participants here are in fact contrasting aspects of a single personality. Augustinus's many strictures reflect the multiple facets of Petrarch's own guilty conscience, just as Franciscus's desires and ambitions mirror his real aspirations. What emerges from the confrontation of almost irreconcilable attitudes is a latent state of mind known to medieval moralists as the sin of sloth, or *accidie*, but which we might feel more inclined to identify as an illness, depression. Nothing pleases Franciscus, except, secretly, the spectacle of his own unhappiness; he becomes inert and incapable of decision or action. Augustinus administers psychotherapy of a rather directive kind, and recommends some helpful reading (Cicero, naturally enough), but the real cure is the text: in finding the words to describe his malady, Petrarch reifies it, and even overcomes it. Franciscus does not in the end bow to all Augustinus's injunctions; the poet and scholar survive the crisis of conscience, and the writer's identity momentarily asserts itself, while at the same time ambition and desire are tempered by the recognition that the experience of which they are an essential feature has an ethical and spiritual dimension.

Interestingly, much of Augustinus's attack in the second book is directed at Franciscus's intellectual habits: at reading, which leads to arrogance, and at writing, which, apart from being a vehicle for mad ambitions, a part of his quest for fame, is also by its very nature inadequate, since words cannot adequately express the realities they attempt to portray. Nor is this analysis of Petrarch's creative dilemma a superficial one, for Augustinus deliberately uses the evidence of Petrarch's own writings (and notably the *Africa*) to prove to Franciscus how arrogant he is; he even chides him for one of his most persistent literary devices, the use of examples borrowed from antiquity.

But, as we saw in the last chapter, the real focus of the father confessor's animus is the wayward son's love, which he condemns as one of the two adamantine chains (the other being ambition) which hold Franciscus captive in his state of sin. The greater part of the third day of the debate is focused upon what Franciscus at first refuses to see as anything but a fine and virtuous predilection, but what Augustinus, following among others 'our' Cicero, as he calls him, condemns as the fiercest of the passions: a misplaced desire for an earthly creature, and an obstacle to the love of the Creator.

In the course of their argument, Augustinus rehearses many of the major lyric themes of the *Canzoniere*, using them as evidence against Franciscus: the passing of time, the effects of age on Laura's beauty, and her premature death which leaves her lover alone. He even points to the literary conceit which is such a central part of Petrarch's personal myth:

> Who can sufficiently condemn the madness of an alienated mind, or be other than amazed when, overcome by the beauty not only of her body but even of her *name*, you have had the incredible vanity to let yourself be led into worshipping everything that sounds the same. You loved the laurel of emperors and poets because that was the name by which she was called, and I do not believe that a single poem flowed from your pen without there being some mention of the laurel in it . . . And in the end, since you could not hope for the imperial laurels, you desired the poetic ones, which the merits of your studies promised you, no less ardently than you desired the woman herself. If you were even now to recall how much effort you put into obtaining them . . . you would be ashamed. (SEC III 158)

It may be, as Petrarch claims in a letter of 1336 (F IV 6) replying to Giacomo Colonna's doubts as to the reality of Laura, that his idea of St Augustine was as much a fiction as his lady love herself (though the ironies are complex and elusive here), but it is clear that the Augustinus of the *Secretum* is a privileged, and complaisant, observer of his creator's psychological processes.

The guilt which is the subject of this inner debate

acquires, by virtue of its literary elaboration, a reality as concrete as that of the ascent of Mont Ventoux: the *Secretum* echoes a profound inner conflict and in so doing makes it a permanent part of the highly structured personality that Petrarch has bequeathed to us. It also reveals the vital influence of a single classical myth not merely upon his writings, but upon his life. The nymph Daphne who was changed into laurels effects an almost Ovidian metamorphosis on the real writer as much as upon the lyric lover of the *Canzoniere*. An early desire to win the unwithering laurels of poetic fame leads not merely to the writing of poetry, but to the re-creation of a classical ceremony of coronation, to imitation not merely in words but in deeds (if indeed the coronation ever took place: apart from Petrarch's accounts, the only independent evidence is provided by Boccaccio, a devoted admirer and outstanding weaver of fictions). The real substance of the Laura whose existence is 'proved' by a brief note in the Virgil manuscript with which our journey began, and by a couple of very literary letters, is her role in the *Canzoniere* and the *Trionfi*: as figure of poetic inspiration, rhetorical ornament and finally moral improvement. Thus when the poet cries that it was she who made her virtue and his passion so famous (C 295), we recognise Petrarch's strategy and Laura's significance: it was rather by writing of her virtue and his passion that he sought to make himself famous.

The same is true of the persistence of the myth in his Latin poetry, for the Daphne of the third eclogue who crowns the poet with laurels, or the laurel of the tenth eclogue whose demise is lamented by Silvanus, are figures of poetry whose function is to enhance the fame of the poet. Indeed so consistent was Petrarch's involvement with this one conceit that he was prepared even to

plant his garden with laurels, and has left us a series of
notes documenting this and other horticultural experi-
ments, unique in their day, in the margin of a manuscript: a genuine personal record as far as we can tell, and
yet still underpinned by reference to the advice of that
great gardener of antiquity, the Virgil of the *Georgics*. In
this homely gesture we witness again the circularity of
life and literature. The private planting of laurels echoes
the public, literary cultivation of their leaves; if the trees
thrive, they will entice Apollo and his Muses into
Petrarch's garden so that he will be inspired to write
poetry there, and they will exemplify that poetic laurel
planted in his heart by love, which is nurtured by his
ploughing pen, the breath of his sighs, and the water of
his tears:

> Amor co la man destra il lato manco
> m'aperse, e piantovvi entro in mezzo 'l core
> un lauro verde si che di colore
> ogni smeraldo avria ben vinto e stanco . . .

> (Love with his right hand opened my left side and planted
> there in the midst of my heart a laurel so green that its
> colour would outshine and weary every emerald . . .)
> (C 228)

When in the tenth eclogue Petrarch assumes the form
of Silvanus, the woodland worshipper and cultivator of
laurels, and declares that the laurel gave him a name and
brought him fame and riches (B X 376–7), it is not hard to
perceive what lies behind the veil of allegory. When he
laments the death of the beloved tree, however, he is
transmuting what may at root have been a genuine
experience—a lady falling victim to the Black Death in
1348—into a literary image located in the densest foliage
of his conceptual tree: an elegy for the passing of all the

poets of antiquity. So that a poetic celebration of the death of Laura provides a pretext for the ultimate demonstration of the poet's erudition enclosed in the allegory of the object of his love: no longer a woman, nor even a tree or a laurel crown, but all the literary laurels of the past. The tenth eclogue is almost the Triumph of Scholarship.

And it is proper (so intricate are the patterns which Petrarch weaves) that Silvanus should be its poet, for silvan solitude is the privileged place of literary composition, as we are reminded by the frontispiece of the Ambrosian Virgil, or repeatedly in the *De vita solitaria*, not least by the example of St Bernard, learning amidst oaks and beeches (vs II 7) or by a letter of 1362 (s I 6) where Petrarch describes himself as 'not so much a scholar as a lover of woodlands, a solitary, given to murmuring foolishly amidst high beeches and, with the utmost presumption, to toying with my little pen beneath a bitter laurel-tree'. In almost all the metamorphoses to which he submits himself, he reveals his essential awareness of writing as the unique mediator of a single composite self.

In the *De vita solitaria*, Petrarch advances three possible reasons for his real love of solitude: his desire to seek the places propitious for literary endeavour, his desire to flee the crowd of mortals with whom (as he so often tells elsewhere) he feels himself to have so little in common, and finally his desire, in full consciousness of the realities of his life, to escape from witnesses who might speak too freely of them (vs I 6). The last urge is revealing, for it betokens not only the self-awareness with which we are by now familiar, but also a jealously guarded autonomy, as much intellectual as moral or social: the freedom to shape himself according to his aspirations regardless of what onlookers might perceive him to be. So that to self-knowledge, and the knowledge of flux and change which are an inevitable concomitant of it, is added the knowledge of the making of the self.

These three levels of awareness are constantly apparent in Petrarch's letters which, precisely because they span the whole of his literary career, and are intended to reflect it, give a sense of duration and chronology to the process of individuation which they both contribute to and record. Asked by his childhood friend Guido Sette to define his state in 1357, Petrarch declares that if state implies stasis, then there is no such thing (F XIX 16); increasingly as the *Familiares* progress, and throughout the *Seniles*, he gives us the sense of a man looking back over his life and perceiving no fixed identity, only change.

Such elusiveness is of course pinned down on occasion, as a habit or character-trait becomes fixed as an enduring image of the man as he wishes us to see him. Scholarship, and the continuation of his studies until his dying day, we already know to be one such element; a minor accompaniment to it, which emerges more strongly as his years go by and his ambitions apparently decline, is the Horatian quest for a modest life: the refusal of high office and rejection of worldly goods or *negotia* which might encroach upon his literary *otium*. But perhaps the most salient characteristic of the correspondence and the man behind it is the urge for friendship: its creation and cultivation in letters, its significance as a literary theme, and its apparently central place in Petrarch's life. By neglecting those friends mentioned in the second chapter, and many others besides, we have chosen to ignore a network of real and literary relationships many of which were as engaging, and long-lasting, as the poetic passion for Laura.

As ever, classical precedents are not far away: Cicero wrote on friendship, and his, and Seneca's, correspondence is largely composed of letters to friends. But life follows art: Petrarch's house was always filled with friends, and so too was his solitude; he often states that it should not entail isolation, and indeed several times tried to persuade friends to settle with him and share it. Furthermore, he assiduously nurtured exchanges of letters, sometimes over several decades, with those to whom he felt close, that closeness transcending distance, absence, and all the vagaries of fortune and passing time. He had also, because of the length of his life and the breadth of his acquaintance, all too frequently to lament the death of friends, the most significant of which he recorded in his Virgil manuscript. The greatest tribute he could pay to them was perhaps to state, as he did in the *De ignorantia*, that perfect friendship entails loving one's friends as oneself (I 1128); dozens of letters bear witness to his efforts to do so, and to his deep awareness of the influential role which friends played in his life and works. It is to them that many of his writings are dedicated, and to them that he addressed most of the texts in which he sought to define the image of himself which he wished to share with them.

Writing is thus both the medium which Petrarch exploits in his efforts to forge an identity for himself and, as we have already seen, a constant topos of those efforts. In his letters as elsewhere there are numerous discussions of the qualities required of a writer, of how and what to write and of the relationship between writing and the innermost mind, as well as of technical matters such as style and imitation, and, naturally, of the works of others. Writing and reading, he repeatedly affirms, are the two greatest of his pleasures, totally absorbing, but totally rewarding: 'of all earthly delights, none is better, none sweeter, none more durable' (s xvii 2). Books are intimate companions rejuvenating him and bringing joy; he expresses his desire for them and his passion for literature in terms borrowed from the language of carnal love, his literary longing far surpassing any more mundane love-affair (e i 6; f xx 14).

Avowals such as these, and many others, reveal the extent to which he was determined to portray himself as writer, and the self-consciousness of his writing. Day and night, and to his dying day, the urge pursues him (f xix 16): 'it is remarkable that I long to write, yet do not know what to write, or to whom' (this in a letter that thus provides its own subject-matter and addressee), 'and yet—what an unrelenting pleasure!—paper, pen, ink and sleepless nights give more satisfaction than sleep and repose' (f xiii 7). Writing is an ingrained habit and a way of life; writing is also, however, a mad passion, a contagious and incurable disease, and a way of death (v 10). Several times he declares he will have no more of it, but it is only in a letter to Boccaccio which he dated 4 June 1373 (though he almost certainly completed it the following year, perhaps only a few weeks before his end), and placed last in the *Seniles*, that he puts a conclusion to his correspondence (s xvii 4). He speaks of the weight of his years, his weariness with all things, and the disgust with and aversion to writing which finally induce him to bid a last epistolary farewell to his friends and, explicitly, to his letters. He might also have added: to himself.

Given so much evidence of Petrarch's self-awareness, but also of his self-concealment, it is hardly fruitful to attempt to separate some notional kernel of fact from the ubiquitous shell of fiction. But one should not suppose that fiction necessarily betokens untruth; it is rather an artful arrangement of the truth. Indeed in a letter of 1370 (s XII 2) Petrarch explains that the task of poets is *fingere*, to invent or fashion, not in the sense of telling lies, but in that of composing and ornamenting, skilfully suggesting the truth by means of artifice and style whilst yet concealing it behind a pleasing veil of fiction. For the poet, it is the finished work of art that is important.

But for the writer in search of an identity, the truth is also essential. In the *De vita solitaria*, Petrarch describes his quest for it in almost diffident terms: 'I do not wish to be a bold asserter of the truth so much as a punctilious seeker after it. Although I always aspire to it zealously, I fear that at times either the recesses in which it hides, or my preoccupations, or some dullness of my wits, hinder me, so that when I am looking for the facts, I become entangled in mere opinions' (VS II 588). Yet the search is frequently alluded to in his letters, and is the keynote to his scholarly investigations of the world of ancient Rome, as witness his many annotations in the margins of the works of the historians. Not for nothing is the debate in the *Secretum* carried on in the presence of Truth, who punctiliously informs us in her opening remarks that Petrarch has portrayed her in the *Africa*, and then silently sits in judgement on every word that is spoken: the truth for which Augustinus and Franciscus are struggling is more important than the cut and thrust of their discussion.

Yet there is no single truth, for what their argument is about, and what Petrarch is thus debating within himself, is the conflict between the revealed truth of religion and the experienced truth of human existence; what emerges from their confrontation, and from many of his letters, is that, in the absence of certainty in this life, it is better to will the good than to know the truth. As his works evolve in his later years into increasingly complex patterns of autobiographical structuring, this motif, the struggle for salvation, becomes dominant; gone is the arrogance of the younger poet, or lover, or scholar, to be replaced by a new consciousness of doubt and ignorance.

So much introspection might lead us to expect a definitive work of autobiography. But there was none. The *Letter to Posterity*, which was intended to round off the *Seniles*, and to which we shall return in our final chapter, remained incomplete. Instead, the whole corpus of Petrarch's writing constitutes a vast, diffuse and constantly evolving portrait of the self, not exactly idealised, but seen through so many different prisms as to become almost kaleidoscopic. The poetic imaginings and lyric outpourings of the *Canzoniere* can be balanced by the scholar-moralist's ordering of the same range of experience in the *Trionfi*; neither represents a spontaneous confession, yet both enclose a fiction important for an understanding of their maker, a fiction given a further learned dimension in the *Bucolicum carmen*. The apparently ruthless self-analysis of the *Secretum* brings all those strands together and yet does not resolve them, deepening our impression of a man who knows himself yet does not know what he wants. The letter-collections above all reflect the interaction of ideals and daily life, of literary posturing and genuine self-questioning: the very first of the *Familiares*, looking back over the correspondence of earlier years which it introduces, posits introspection as a vital activity, and the habit persists right through the collection and, with increasing frequency, in the *Seniles*. Even certain of the metrical

Epistole contain important passages of autobiographical description or reminiscence.

Petrarch's desire to sum himself up is, not surprisingly in view of his age, most evident in the last eight years of his life. Half a dozen of the *Seniles* written after 1366 reveal his preoccupation with his life-story; he certainly worked on the *Letter to Posterity* during this period, and the *De ignorantia* too contains a substantial account of his past (I 1052–6). What emerges most strongly from these late texts is his sense of then and now, of what he had been and what he had become, or at least what he wanted to become in the eyes of those who would come after. For it is the ultimate proof of Petrarch's deliberate structuring of himself that he had his eye firmly fixed upon posterity.

The justification for such aspirations no doubt derives in part from his consciousness of the role of the historian, evoked in the prologue to the *De viris illustribus*: to transmit the lessons of the past and the examples of great men to the present, and indeed the future. But in addition he was clearly concerned himself to become one of those great men, as Augustinus points out when he accuses Franciscus of devoting all his energies to the *Africa* and *De viris illustribus* in order to win favour with posterity, and thereby of neglecting himself (SEC III 192). He was inordinately preoccupied with what others thought of him (however much he denies the fact); the *De ignorantia* is only the latest of a series of texts which he wrote to defend himself against critics. The only criticism which was allowed to stand, and even then not entirely to prevail, was that to which Augustinus gave voice: his own perception of his own blemishes, artfully conserved for generations to come.

'Early manhood led me astray, maturity swept me

away, but old age set me straight' (P 2). This is how Petrarch presents himself in the *Letter to Posterity*, and this is how he wished to see himself. But, as we have been able to observe, his peculiarly elusive character, far from resolving itself into so epigrammatic a formula, was the subject, and the object, of an immensely complex work of art. Were there no other, that would be his legacy to us.

7 The afterlife

Posterity also has other reasons to be grateful to Petrarch. Not least, for his awareness of its very existence; the consciousness that his own story was developing over time carried with it the realisation that this development would continue into the future, that his image would vary according to the diversity of men's views, and that in one sense therefore his life was not his own. In a letter deploring the state of Avignon (SN 6) he sets out his polemical stand in terms which are almost a paradigm of his literary existence: 'I will write, Truth will dictate, and the whole human race will bear witness. You, posterity, must judge . . .'. This concern with the verdict of the future, coupled with a desire for the durable fame which it alone could bring, marks almost all his writings. It is often expressed in strategic positions such as the preface to the *De viris illustribus* or the opening letter of the *Familiares*, but is also rehearsed in the *Canzoniere* and the *Trionfi*, often coupled with the admission that such aspirations are vain; it is equally a major theme of Augustinus's criticism in the *Secretum*, and even makes its presence felt in the Coronation Oration, there undoubtedly owing its origins to Cicero's view of the poet in his *Pro Archia*, which Petrarch had discovered in 1333.

The two most striking instances of this topic occur, however, in the *Africa* and the *Letter to Posterity*. In the ninth book of the epic, the poet Ennius tells the hero Scipio of his future fame. Just as Achilles was sung of by Homer, he says, so Scipio too will have his own poet.

Describing the art of poetry and the laurels which symbolise it, he then goes on to relate a dream in which Homer appears to him and reveals the poets of the future, one of whom is a young Tuscan resting in an enclosed valley (Vaucluse) beneath a laurel-tree, pen in hand (like Virgil in Simone Martini's miniature), and is called Franciscus. He will sing the praises of Scipio in his *Africa*; he will be crowned with laurels on the Capitoline; he will be the greatest poet for ten centuries, and will write of the lives of the men of ancient Rome; who can tell what plans his fertile mind is not contemplating? And finally, before Ennius awakes, Homer remarks upon the young Franciscus's love of the countryside, his travels, and the writing that he will do when freed from the whirl of worldly affairs (A IX 278–89).

As if this were not sufficient, Petrarch proceeds to relate Scipio's triumphal coronation with laurels on the Capitoline, with the poet Ennius similarly crowned beside him, and then turns to bid his poem farewell, evoking his efforts, fifteen centuries on, to trace and to imitate the heroes of antiquity with the same leaves, in the same place, and with the same glorious name, lest Homer's prophecy of him might prove of no avail (A IX 387–409). He commends his *Africa* to posterity, however gloomy the immediate future may appear, and trusts that it will preserve the exploits it records—his own as much as Scipio's—beyond his death and to eternity (A IX 421–83). Had we no other proof of Petrarch's self-consciousness, and of the way in which he cast himself as his own hero, this remarkably arrogant conclusion to his boldest and ironically most incomplete literary enterprise would surely provide it. We are reminded once again of the dwarf who is determined to see further than the giants on whose shoulders he is perched: Petrarch's imitation of antiquity is evidently intended to transcend it.

Yet the *Africa* was substantially a work of the earlier part of his career, and to find what he no doubt intended to be the older and wiser man's view of himself, and perhaps the definitive one, we must turn to the *Letter to Posterity*, planned to complete and close the collection of *Seniles*. It is, like so many of Petrarch's writings, open-ended and unresolved. It tells of the events of his life up to 1351, and may well have begun as an apologia for his long stay with the Visconti in Milan, yet it probably only took shape over the course of the following fifteen years, and was significantly enlarged and retouched in 1370–1. It is literally addressed to posterity.

It opens with a thumbnail sketch of its author, seen across time and in the moralist's perspective of the wisdom of old age recognising the vanity of youth. He had been bright-eyed, good-looking and healthy, had despised wealth and its excesses, had preferred to eat with friends rather than alone, and had suffered the pangs of love, physical pangs. He had not been proud, but was sometimes angry; he had sought friendship with all manner of men and had cultivated it loyally. He was of modest intelligence and devoted to his research, especially that into moral philosophy and poetry, though with time he had abandoned the latter in favour of the holy scriptures. He was fascinated by antiquity, and notably by its historians; he would have preferred to have been born in an earlier age. He enjoyed conversation, but did not regard it as a proper cause for fame: he wished to be remembered for having lived righteously (P 2–6).

There follows an account of the major events of his career: his studies, travels, retreat to Vaucluse and, occupying a disproportionate part of the story, his coronation. Some of his Latin works are mentioned, but of the *Canzoniere* there is no word. At each stage, he is careful to correlate letters he wrote and placed in his collections with the events to which they bear witness. The picture is coherently composed, even if incomplete: a portrait of Petrarch as he wished to be remembered, with the supporting evidence of the texts he wished to preserve. In an age singularly ill-provided with autobiographies, the project was a unique conclusion to a whole life of self-structuring, and the particular awareness of the future which it betokened was exceptional.

For Petrarch perceived himself at a pivotal point in time: his *Familiares* conclude with letters addressed to the great writers of antiquity and thus look back into the classical past; his *Seniles* seek their conclusion, as we have seen, in letters looking forward to the future. Similarly, the *Africa* recalls the glories of the past not merely for the present, but for posterity; the *De viris illustribus* is designed, less poetically, with the same intention, and in the *Rerum memorandarum libri* Petrarch even states that he is like a man standing on the boundary between two peoples, looking both forwards and backwards (RM I 19). To make of this declaration the first modern historiographical perception of the existence of a Middle Ages now past is to ignore the context: it is not so much that he looks back to the Dark Ages and forwards to the illumination of the Renaissance, as that he looks back to the authors of the classical age, and forwards to a possibly ignorant posterity which will care nothing for them. In this sense, in his awareness and his cultivation of his own literary-historical position, Petrarch is indeed a key figure, for in his self-conscious symbiosis with antiquity he was to bequeath to the future an approach to and knowledge of his own literary heritage which would ensure that the posterity he perceived would be less ignorant than he feared. Only thus, by identifying with the great men of the past and measuring their experience against his own, could he finally triumph over time.

But what of Petrarch's literary legacy, and what has posterity made of him? The ironies are manifold. If they have heard of Petrarch at all, most people nowadays know him as a writer of Italian sonnets and the lover of Laura, as if all his disclaimers (however disingenuous) of his 'vernacular fragments' had been in vain. What he himself undoubtedly regarded as the major part of his achievement, that body of Latin writing which accounts for more than nine-tenths of his surviving work, has been largely forgotten until recently. And of his scholarship only scholars are aware, having some cause to be grateful for it.

Had it not been for the pioneering philological work which he accomplished, our knowledge of classical texts would in all probability be poorer than it is. The contribution which he made to the rediscovery and transmission of Roman literature, whatever his short-comings as a scholar viewed with six centuries of hindsight, was a significant element in that recovery of the ancient world which was to be a feature of the Renaissance; a century after his death, his first northern biographer, the Dutch humanist Rudolph Agricola, could speak of him as the initiator of humane studies, to whom all the erudition of his age was owed, the liberator and restorer of classical letters. It is a minor tragedy that his library, which, ever mindful of posterity, he had at one stage intended to bequeath to the city of Venice as the first public library of European history, was on the contrary dispersed on his death and is only slowly being pieced together today. It was to his books, his dearest companions, his Cicero and his Virgil, that he confided the choicest fruits of his erudition, and many of these are lost.

But his learning informed all his Latin writings, and it was these, written in a language which knew no national barriers, which first earned him his laurels, not only on the Capitoline in 1341, but throughout Europe, and for many years to come. In his lifetime, these works brought him real renown as a scholar, writer and moralist: he became a public figure of international repute and his writings were in constant demand, sometimes even before he had completed them. After his death, his reputation did not cease to grow: there are still in existence today more than 500 manuscript copies of his various Latin works, attesting their popularity and diffusion beyond the frontiers of Italy in the late fourteenth and fifteenth centuries. By the time that printing was introduced in the 1460s, they were being read in places as far-flung as York, Stockholm, Cracow, Ragusa and Alcobaça; the new technology opened the way for numerous editions, culminating, but not coming to an end, in the *Opera omnia* printed in Basle in 1554 and 1581. Significantly, the single work for which demand was highest all over Europe was undoubtedly the *De remediis* which, together with his extremely popular Latin translation of the Griselda story (s XVII 4), guaranteed Petrarch the image of a moralist, and one whose teaching is copiously illustrated by the examples of antiquity.

Given the stoic colouring of his treatise on Fortune, it would be tempting to suppose that Petrarch, through its diffusion, played a special role in the rebirth of Stoicism which was to characterise Renaissance thought. But the contrary appears likely: rather, the *De remediis* was read, or consulted, for the orthodox moral views which it reflected, for its commonplace (if often classical) consolations and its stern warnings. That certain likeminded men perceived Petrarch's particular message is possible, but these men were rare, and belong to the ranks of those whom we now label early humanists. To such men, a generation younger than Petrarch in Italy, and two or three generations younger in France and elsewhere, his name was one to be conjured with, and his writings were sources of the most intense interest. Ironically, however, one of the most popular themes of Petrarch's moral thinking was precisely that most at variance with his lyric creativity: the traditional clerical antifeminism expounded in both books of the *De remediis*.

In Italy, however, the poetic laurels also thrived from the beginning. Petrarch himself had been aware of the geographical limitations of his mother tongue (c 146); the *Canzoniere*, and indeed the *Trionfi*, could not initially travel beyond the Alps, except possibly to Spain, for the simple reason that they would not be understood. But on their native soil they engendered a vast profusion of vernacular verse coming at first under the moral sway of the *Trionfi*, then under the lyric inspiration of the sonnets and *canzoni* and especially of the structure into which they had been formed. The imitation now known as Petrarchism became a major poetic phenomenon, initially in Italy and subsequently all over Europe.

The first signs of an interest in the *Trionfi* beyond the Alps may be detected in France in the 1470s, and are very much in accord with the image of the moralist forged by the Latin works which had preceded them by the best part a century; it is not until some sixty or seventy years later that the lyrics begin to be translated or imitated, and by that time the imitation is often at second hand, the poets of the Pléiade drawing as much on Petrarchists as on Petrarch himself. In England, with the sole exception of a translation, possibly not direct from the Italian, of the sonnet 'S'amor non è che dunque è quel ch'io sento?' (c 132) which Chaucer inserted into his *Troilus and Criseyde* in the 1380s, there is no sign of any interest in the *Canzoniere* before 1527, when Thomas Wyatt, returning from Italy, translated and adapted several of its poems. Yet in the preceding century and a half, the Latin works, and even by the beginning of the sixteenth century the *Trionfi*, were known, admired and imitated. The *Trionfi*, too, were to have a remarkable impact upon the visual arts, providing subject-matter in particular for decorative painting, and for tapestries such as those now preserved at Hampton Court.

Wherever one looks in Europe, the same pattern emerges: first, the overwhelming success of the Latin works, then, confirming the image of the moralist, the rise of the *Trionfi*, and finally, above all in the sixteenth century, the triumph of the *Canzoniere*. Today, Petrarch's love-poetry is an international currency: it has been translated into and imitated in Catalan, Spanish, Portuguese, French, English, Scottish, Flemish, Dutch, German, Dalmatian, Hungarian, Polish, Russian and Cypriot Greek, and doubtless other languages as well. The posterity which Petrarch seems not to have anticipated has judged his vernacular fragments more kindly than ever he dared openly to hope.

'Perhaps you will have heard something of me', he opens his Letter to Posterity with evident false modesty, 'though it is doubtful whether my obscure little name will have been able to come down to you across space and time. And perhaps you will want to know what kind of a man I was, and what has become of my works, especially those of which you have heard tell, however vaguely' (P 2). In so brief a conspectus as this, we have seen his ultimate aspiration fulfilled: if in the end we do not know what kind of a man he was, we can see what kind of a man he wished himself to be, and we, like every generation of his posterity, can make of his works what we wish to make of them.

Petrarch is sometimes called the father of humanism, and there is no doubt that in the amalgam of pagan and Christian, of classical scholarship and a dual consciousness of human frailty and human potential which we find everywhere in his work, he gives to that term something of its modern meaning. He has been called the first modern historian; his attempts to plant trees mark him as an early exponent of the experimental method and have earned him the label of first modern gardener; his ascent of Mont Ventoux has been hailed, however erroneously, as the first act of modern mountaineering. He was besides as we have seen a traveller, a diplomat, a moralist and a man who valued friendship highly. Above all, however, in his perception of himself, in his acute awareness of his inner motives, and in his never-ceasing efforts to construct an image of himself for posterity, we might consider him the first modern man. That image must be recaptured from the whole range of his writings, but as he recedes into the tree-lined fourteenth-century landscape of Simone Martini's miniature, pen in hand, he lingers in the mind's eye incarnate in that Virgilian vision: as poet, as scholar-exegete, and as his own several heroes.

Abbreviations

References to those of Petrarch's works which are frequently mentioned in the pages above are indicated by the following abbreviations; the full titles of the works, the editions used and translations available are listed together with suggestions for further reading in the pages that follow. All translations in the text are my own.

A	*Africa*
B	*Bucolicum carmen*
C	*Canzoniere*
E	*Epistole (metrice)*
F	*Familiares*
I	*De ignorantia*
OR	*De otio religioso*
P	*Posteritati*
RF	*De remediis utriusque fortune*
RM	*Rerum memorandarum libri*
S	*Seniles*
SEC	*Secretum*
SN	*Sine nomine*
T	*Testamentum*
TM	*Triumphus mortis*
TT	*Triumphus temporis*
V	*Epistolae variae*
VI	*De viris illustribus*
VS	*De vita solitaria*

Further reading

This book is neither a detailed account of Petrarch's life nor a systematic analysis of his works, but an attempt to present both life and works as complementary creations of a single elusive intellect. Like those dwarfs astride the shoulders of giants who made their first appearance in Chapter 2, it rests heavily upon the labours of others, and what follows is intended to guide the reader curious to see further to the giants who will make that possible.

1. *Editions.* There is no complete modern edition of Petrarch's works. For some, reference has to be made to the 1554 Basle edition (*Francisci Petrarchae opera*, 3 vols, referred to below as *Opera 1554*). The most recent or most readily accessible reliable editions of the writings mentioned in this study (together with an English translation, where one exists; in one or two cases the edition used is a bilingual one) are listed below in the alphabetical order of the abbreviations used to identify them. Three partial editions, all of them with Italian parallel translations for the Latin texts, will be referred to in addition to *Opera 1554*:

Opere: Opere latine di Francesco Petrarca, ed. A. Buffano, 2 vols, Turin 1975; *Prose: Francesco Petrarca, Prose*, ed. G. Martellotti *et al.*, Milan–Naples 1955; *Rime: Francesco Petrarca, Rime, Trionfi e poesie latine*, ed. F. Neri *et al.*, Milan–Naples 1951.

Africa, ed. N. Festa, Florence 1926; *Petrarch's Africa*, trans. and ann. T. G. Bergin and A. S. Wilson, New Haven–London 1977 (A)

Petrarch's Bucolicum carmen, trans. and ann. T. G. Bergin, New Haven–London 1974 (B)

Canzoniere (*Rerum vulgarium fragmenta*): in *Rime*, 3–477; *Petrarch's Lyric Poems*, trans. and ed. R. M. Durling, Cambridge, Mass.–London 1976 (C)

Coronation Oration (*Collatio laureationis*): in *Opere*, II 1255–83; trans. in E. H. Wilkins, *Studies in the Life and Works of Petrarch*, Cambridge, Mass. 1955

Epistole (*metrice*): *Francisci Petrarchae poemata minora* ..., II–III, ed. D. Rossetti, Milan 1829–34 (E)

Familiarium rerum libri: *Le familiari*, 4 vols, ed. V. Rossi, Florence 1933–42; *Rerum familiarium libri I–VIII*, trans. A. S. Bernardo, Albany, N.Y. 1975; *Letters on Familiar Matters, IX–XVI*, trans. A. S. Bernardo, Baltimore–London 1982 (F)

Griselda (*De insigni obedientia et fide uxoria*) (*Seniles* XVII 4), in
  Opere, II 1311–39

De ignorantia: *De sui ipsius et multorum ignorantia* in *Opere*, II
  1025–1151; *On His Own Ignorance*, trans. H. Nachod in E.
  Cassirer *et al*., eds, *The Renaissance Philosophy of Man*,
  Chicago 1948, 49–133 (I)

Invectiva contra Gallum: *Invectiva contra eum qui maledixit
  Italie*, in *Opere*, II 1153–253

Invectiva contra medicum, in *Opere*, II 817–981

*Invectiva contra quendam magni status hominem sed nulli
  scientie aut virtutis*, in *Opere*, II 983–1023

Itinerarium ad sepulcrum domini nostri Jesu Cristi, ed. G.
  Lumbroso in *Memorie italiane del buon tempo antico*, Turin
  1889, 16–49

De otio religioso, in *Opere*, I 567–809 (OR)

Posteritati (*Seniles* XVIII 1), in *Prose*, 2–19 (P)

Psalmi penitentiales: *Pétrarque, les psaumes pénitentiaux*, ed. H.
  Cochin, Paris 1929

De remediis utriusque fortune, in *Opera* 1554, I 1–254; *Physike
  against Fortune, as well prosperous as adverse*, trans. Thomas
  Twyne, London 1559 (RF)

Rerum memorandarum libri, ed. G. Billanovich, Florence 1943 (RM)

Seniles: *Epistole rerum senilium*, in *Opera* 1554, II 812–1070 (S)

Secretum: *De secreto conflictu curarum mearum*, in *Prose*,
  22–215; *Petrarch's Secret, or the Soul's Conflict with Passion*,
  trans. W. H. Draper, London 1911 (SEC)

Sine nomine. Lettere polemiche e politiche, ed. U. Dotti, Rome–
  Bari 1974; *Petrarch's Book Without a Name*, trans. N. P.
  Zacour, Toronto 1973 (SN)

Speech to Jean le Bon: *Collatio coram domino Iohanne Francorum
  rege*, in *Opere*, II 1285–1309

Petrarch's Testament, ed. and trans. T. E. Mommsen, Ithaca 1957 (T)

Trionfi, in *Rime*, 481–559; *The Triumphs of Petrarch*, trans. E. H.
  Wilkins, Chicago 1962 (TM, TT)

Epistolae variae, ed. G. Fracassetti, in *Epistulae de rebus famili-
  aribus et variae*, III, Florence 1863, 309–488 (V)

De viris illustribus, ed. G. Martellotti, Florence 1964 (VI)

De vita solitaria, in *Prose*, 286–591; *The Life of Solitude*, trans. J.
  Zeitlin, Urbana, Ill. 1924 (VS)

In addition, three anthologies containing a good number of texts in translation may be noted:

E. H. R. Tatham, *Francesco Petrarca, The First Modern Man of Letters*, 2 vols, London 1925–6; J. H. Robinson and H. W. Rolfe, *Petrarch: The First Modern Scholar and Man of Letters*, 2nd ed., New York 1914; D. B. Thompson, *Petrarch, a Humanist among Princes*, New York 1971.

2. *Manuscripts*. All research into Petrarch's intellectual life depends to a large extent upon the evidence of his autograph manuscripts and of manuscripts from his library. His Virgil and Livy, which have received particular mention in this study, are available in facsimile:

Francisci Petrarcae Vergilianus Codex, ed. G. Galbiati, Milan 1930 (Milan, Biblioteca Ambrosiana, MS S.P. Arm. 10, scat. 27); G. Billanovich, *La tradizione del testo di Livio e le origini dell'-umanesimo*, II, *Il Livio del Petrarca e del Valla*, Padua 1981 (London, British Library, MS Harley 2493).

In the absence of a comprehensive list either of the autographs or of books belonging to Petrarch, the reader should consult A. Petrucci, *La scrittura di Francesco Petrarca*, Vatican City 1967, 115–29.

3. *Studies*. There is no comprehensive and up-to-date guide to the very considerable number of books and articles devoted to Petrarch and his works. A. E. Quaglio, *Francesco Petrarca*, Milan 1967, 197–234, offers, however, a valuable survey of the most important material; see also B. Corrigan, 'Petrarch in English', *Italica*, 50 (1973), 400–7. The journals *Studi Petrarcheschi* and *Italia medio-evale e umanistica* should also be consulted; the latter has in recent years contained many significant contributions to Petrarchan studies, including catalogues of manuscripts. The annual bibliographies in *The Year's Work in Modern Language Studies* and *Italian Studies* are also most useful.

The standard short biography in English is E. H. Wilkins, *Life of Petrarch*, Chicago–London 1961, based upon several much more detailed studies by the same author. The almost impeccable biographical bones which it offers have a great deal of elegant and entertaining (but not always reliable) flesh added to them by M. Bishop, *Petrarch and his World*, Bloomington, Ind. 1963.

A starting-point (though now somewhat outdated) for any serious knowledge of Petrarch's classical reading and its impact upon his intellectual life is P. de Nolhac, *Pétrarque et l'humanisme*, 2nd ed., Paris 1907, but the grand master of this area of modern Petrarchan scholarship is undoubtedly Giuseppe Billanovich, most of whose work is concealed in articles in learned periodicals (e.g. his 'Petrarch and the textual tradition of Livy', *Journal of the Warburg and Courtauld Institutes*, 14 (1951), 137–208). His *Petrarca letterato. I. Lo Scrittoio del Petrarca*, Rome 1947, is essential reading. There are two important articles by H. Baron on the evolution of Petrarch's thought and the revision of the *Secretum* in his *From Petrarch to Leonardo Bruni*, Chicago 1968, 7–101. On the latter question, the latest study is, however, in Spanish: F. Rico, *Vita u obra de Petrarca, I. Lectura del Secretum*, Padua 1974. Other aspects of Petrarch's intellectual life and their cultural context are explored by J. H. Whitfield, *Petrarch and the Renascence*, Oxford 1943, and C. Trinkaus, *Petrarch and the Formation of the Renaissance Consciousness*, New Haven–London 1979. On his writing in particular, there are brilliant studies of detail by G. Contini in his *Varianti e altra linguistica*, Turin 1970, and a stimulating and more speculative approach to the Latin works by A. Tripet: *Pétrarque ou la connaissance de soi*, Geneva 1967.

The evolution of his vernacular lyrics has received close attention from a number of scholars, and most notably E. H. Wilkins, *The Making of the Canzoniere and Other Petrarchan Studies*, Rome 1951; Wilkins has also produced indispensable guides to his letters: *Petrarch's Correspondence*, Padua 1960, and *The Epistolae Metricae of Petrarch. A Manual*, Rome 1956.

Studies in English of individual works include two volumes by A. S. Bernardo: *Petrarch, Scipio and the Africa*, Baltimore 1962, and *Petrarch, Laura and the Triumphs*, Albany, N.Y. 1974. There are a number of important and interesting articles in two recent commemorative volumes: *Francis Petrarch Six Centuries Later*, ed. A. Scaglione, Chapel Hill 1975, and *Francesco Petrarca Citizen of the World*, Padua–Albany 1980.

The critical literature of Petrarchism is vast. S. Minta, *Petrarch and Petrarchism. The English and French Traditions*, Manchester 1980, is a helpful introductory guide, and L. W. Foster, *The Icy Fire: Five Studies in European Petrarchism*, Cambridge 1969, an elegant illustration. English translations of the lyrics are listed in G. Watson, *The English Petrarchans*, London 1967.

Index

Index